MW01201153

Praise for *Lead Extraordinary Change*

"As SVP of product development at Intuit, Mamie drove extraordinary transformation of team, process, and product. She took over a group that was behind and resistant to change, and up-leveled and inspired the team, modernized their processes, modernized their technology, got them innovating architecture and features, moved them to web and then cloud, ultimately passing the competition by. Mamie has codified her approaches in her new book, *Lead Extraordinary Change*. It's an engaging read and a proven playbook."

—Tayloe Stansbury, CEO, Kaleidescape; Former CTO, Intuit

"Mamie Jones is an exceptional leader who has successfully driven transformational change by mastering the art of hearts and minds leadership. She excels in communicating a burning platform, ensuring that her teams not only understand but deeply feel the urgency for change. Mamie's ability to foster shared consciousness on the direction of the transformation and to engage expansive teams, where the collective "we" is stronger than "me," has consistently led to extraordinary outcomes. Her leadership journey is a testament to her visionary approach and her unwavering commitment to bringing about positive change through the playbook and experiences she shares in this book."

—Cece Morken, Former CEO, Headspace; Former EVP GM, Intuit

"I've had the privilege of witnessing exemplary leadership from Mamie firsthand. Her ability to inspire, guide, and bring out the best in the team is unparalleled. She is a true leader who leads with vision, integrity, and a relentless commitment to excellence. I am truly inspired by the book *Lead Extraordinary Change*. It provides invaluable insights and practical strategies that empower leaders to navigate and drive transformative journeys. A must-read for anyone seeking to make a lasting impact in today's dynamic world."

—Ravi Metta, Former VP, Intuit ProTax Group

"Apart from codifying a repeatable and actionable playbook for organizational transformation, Mamie has sprinkled in several nuggets of career advice for leaders with growth aspirations. She manages to amalgamate key learnings from several renowned leadership books with her own career experiences seamlessly. Through her humility and easy-to-read narration, Mamie manages to build confidence and inspire action for her readers."

—Vinod Periagaram, Former VP, Intuit

LEAD
EXTRAORDINARY
CHANGE

LEAD EXTRAORDINARY CHANGE

The PROVEN PLAYBOOK for **CHANGE**

DRIVING SUCCESSFUL ORGANIZATIONAL TRANSFORMATION

MAMIE F. JONES

Forbes | Books

Copyright © 2024 by Mamie F. Jones.

All rights reserved. No part of this book may be used or reproduced in any manner whatsoever without prior written consent of the author, except as provided by the United States of America copyright law.

Published by Forbes Books, Charleston, South Carolina. Member of Advantage Media.

Forbes Books is a registered trademark, and the Forbes Books colophon is a trademark of Forbes Media, LLC.

Printed in the United States of America.

10 9 8 7 6 5 4 3 2 1

ISBN: 978-1-95588-492-1 (Hardcover)
ISBN: 978-1-95588-493-8 (eBook)

LCCN: 2024904685

Cover and layout design by Lance Buckley.
Headshot by Kimberly Millard.

This custom publication is intended to provide accurate information and the opinions of the author in regard to the subject matter covered. It is sold with the understanding that the publisher, Forbes Books, is not engaged in rendering legal, financial, or professional services of any kind. If legal advice or other expert assistance is required, the reader is advised to seek the services of a competent professional.

Since 1917, Forbes has remained steadfast in its mission to serve as the defining voice of entrepreneurial capitalism. Forbes Books, launched in 2016 through a partnership with Advantage Media, furthers that aim by helping business and thought leaders bring their stories, passion, and knowledge to the forefront in custom books. Opinions expressed by Forbes Books authors are their own. To be considered for publication, please visit **books.Forbes.com**.

To my dearest parents,
George and Margaret Timmons—extraordinary leaders

Contents

Making It Happen

You don't lead by pointing and telling people some place to go.
You lead by going to that place and making a case.

—KEN KESEY

It's Not All about You

Change happens to all of us, whether we like it or not. So, when it comes to transformation in business, it's hard, and most efforts fail. In fact, thought leader and Harvard Business School professor John Kotter says 70 percent of transformation efforts run aground. (Later studies have shown the number to be as high as 78 percent![1]) How we manage transformation is therefore imperative. If it is done with a proven playbook, passion, and persistence, you can be successful and realize more than you ever could have imagined.

For thirty-five years, I have taken organizations, and more importantly, the *people* of those organizations, through enormous and powerful transformation. Most of the companies I worked for wanted

---

1   Paul A. Argenti, Jenifer Berman, Ryan Calsbeek, and Andrew White-house, "The Secret Behind Successful Corporate Transformations," *Harvard Business Review*, September 2021, https://hbr.org/2021/09/the-secret-behind-successful-corporate-transformations.

to institute dramatic change to improve their organization, surpass their competition, and change the trajectory of their company. Some wanted to pivot to new business models, to drive improved or new revenue models; others wanted to diversify and enter new markets to achieve dramatic growth. What is consistent with successful transformation efforts is the ability of leadership to inspire people to achieve results and lead them to greater heights.

Through my thirty-five years, I have seen success and failure, ups and downs, trial and error, and have documented a proven playbook that works for anyone who wants to drive fundamental change and produce extraordinary results. If you desire to take your organization through a successful transformation that will open new doors for your business, and new doors for you, this playbook will be your guide.

It Starts with You, but It's Not All about You

Transformation centers around people, and to get there, the first person that needs to be the focus is *you*. It's easy to speak about other people who need to change—leaders, managers, and employees—but you have to do the hard work first. My motto has always been "good things take time," and this is true for you and for others that you will bring along this lifelong journey. And believe me, it's worth it.

As I've developed my playbook and documented what works, looking more deeply at my own story while writing this book, I've realized that the starting point consists of five words:

It's not all about you.

It may seem somewhat ironic to say it all starts with you, yet it isn't about you. But it's true. This was a tough lesson for me to learn, but once I learned it, I was propelled further than I ever dreamed.

It was the late '80s, and I was working for Travelocity.com as a new director. I thought I knew how to lead a team and was confident in my leadership abilities. But then one morning I arrived at the office and noticed a book was on my desk.

"I wonder what this is," I thought as I settled in my office.

It was Stephen R. Covey's book *The 7 Habits of Highly Effective People*.

"Hmm," I thought, puzzled. "Someone must have left this here by mistake."

I read the blurb at the back and flipped through some of the pages, wondering why this was here. As I reflected a little more, I quickly realized that this was no mistake. Instead, this was a big hint that maybe I was not the great leader I thought I was.

I'm a very competitive person, and I care immensely about what people think of me. Needless to say, the fact that this book was put on my desk bothered me all day. I was forced to take a good look at myself, my abilities, and my motivations.

Generally, people want to improve their careers but often don't know how or what to do. So, they rely on what they know, and this often shows up as managers/leaders taking credit for work done by others instead of sharing where credit is due. This is a common mistake. Before this pivotal point in my development, I saw leadership as pretty much all about me. Sure, it involved people, but I was put in the position of leadership, and I thought ultimately it was all about how successfully I could manage the team. Their performance was essentially on my shoulders, which would affect *my* career and how *I* would achieve success. I was focused on *my* career, *my* talent, and *my* abilities and how *I* came across to others in the organization.

Well, I needed a wake-up call, and someone gave me the shove that was necessary. They had the courage to give me some tough love.

There is some history to my behavior and leadership during this time. In my younger years, I thrived in competitive environments. In school I excelled in academics, music, and sports. I participated in gymnastics, track and field, and springboard diving—always coming in first or second in my events. I was first chair of my woodwind section, made the honor roll, held track and field records, came in first all around in gymnastics, and in my early twenties was ranked twenty-first in diving for the United States. I was used to winning.

You might notice that the recurring pattern of my life is I never really played team sports or, quite frankly, team anything. I suppose at the time I just never thought about it. I seemed to prefer those sports where I was in control of my own outcomes and ability to win. I relied on myself for success or failure. Growing up around the Portland, Oregon, area, I was the youngest of four and was always trying to keep up with my older siblings, which I'm sure helped shape my competitive spirit.

What I lacked was keen self-awareness, which is essential for leaders to succeed. This is often referred to as emotional intelligence—and some people come by this naturally while others must develop the skill. I needed to realize that it was not about me but that leadership was about *people*. Receiving a book anonymously that basically tells you that *you suck* is the kind of experience that has the potential to bring you down and keep you down—if you don't learn from it. But everything in life is about perspective. For me, it was the catalyst that set me on my leadership journey. And what a journey it has been!

As I've gone through the United States speaking on leading trans-formational change and presenting my playbook, I tend to get two types of people coming up to me afterward. The first is women. They want to know how I, as a woman, managed to rise through the ranks and play a senior vice president role for companies like Intuit, Dun & Bradstreet, and Sabre/Travelocity.com. They have dreams and aspirations, just as I did, and want to know what I have done differently. How have I navigated these treacherous waters?

The second includes both men and women who are embarking on, or are in the midst of, a transformation and are seeking help. "I enjoyed the talk," they say after hearing me speak. "But what else can you tell me? My situation is different from yours."

Regardless what you're looking for, I want to simply say, if I can do it, you can too.

Once I graduated college with an education degree, I didn't really know what I wanted to do with my life. I did well in sports, but I knew that was not going to be part of my future career endeavors. So, I thought about music. Music was important to me, thanks to my parents, George and Margaret Timmons, both musicians. George was the assistant dean of education at Portland State University, but music was always his passion. He led a six-piece dance band, mostly on the weekends, and played up to fifty gigs a year, so from a young age, there was always music in our home. My mom was also a pianist, and all my siblings played at least one instrument. My primary musical instrument was the flute, and I went to Boston University to take lessons from the first chair of the Boston Symphony. But I soon realized through this experience that being a professional musician was not my calling. I found it very limiting and confining because *hours* of my time were spent in practice rooms, not an upbeat and fun place to be!

Because I graduated with an education degree and possessed skills in athletics and music, I was recruited for a K–8 teaching position.

I taught for two years and realized that was not my passion either. During this time, my dad would frequently quote to me this famous line from the renowned microbiologist, Louis Pasteur: "Fortune favors the prepared mind."[2] I knew education was important, and so I earned my master's degree over my two years of teaching. I was preparing for whatever would come my way, and as you will see, this served me very well down the road, even if at the time I didn't really know exactly what it would do for me.

"If you prepare yourself, when those serendipitous opportunities arise, you can take a swing," my dad would remind me.

My dad also had a passion for leadership and used to read a lot of Peter Drucker, the famous management consultant who wrote almost forty books and coined the term "knowledge worker"[3] (high-level workers who apply theoretical and analytical knowledge). I think my dad got the Pasteur quote from Drucker, as Drucker liked to quote it too, apparently. A lot of my father's insights and little sayings prepared me for what was going to unfold in my life. We would have many conversations about leadership at home; my dad really enjoyed that sort of discussion. Whether or not I knew it, he was probably planting seeds for me to see leadership differently.

At the end of my second year of teaching, I had the opportunity to emigrate to Australia. I developed a close relationship with an Australian man and made the decision to join him in Adelaide, Australia. He helped me land a job managing a fitness center and helped me to obtain my resident visa. While I loved Australia, my prospects for advancement were extremely limited, and my relationship was not panning out. So after a year I made the decision to come back to the

---

2   Louis Pasteur, "Lecture as Dean of the New Faculty of Sciences," University of Lille, December 7, 1854.

3   P. F. Drucker, *The Landmarks of Tomorrow* (New York: Harper and Row, 1959), 93.

US, returning to Oregon. I needed to find a job, and because I had experience in retail as a younger person, I interviewed and was hired by Nordstrom. I did very well and was on my way to becoming a buyer for one of their departments, but that meant working holidays and weekends, which I wasn't willing to do long term. During this time, I met and married my first husband, and we had three children in basically one year.

How do you have three children in nearly a year? Well, first came my son, and a year and four days later, twin girls!

Our son was born in Oregon, and then we moved to Washington, DC, where our two daughters were born. For four years we lived in DC and then moved to Fort Worth, Texas. Each time we moved, it was because of a work transfer for my husband. So I was doing the rather typical thing at the time, moving around as my husband built his career. I was fine with that, as it allowed me time to be with my children in their formative years. But to keep busy, in DC I took part-time jobs working at Neiman Marcus and coached soccer and springboard diving at the National Cathedral School. I was never one to be idle.

In Fort Worth, my husband was the general manager of the Hyatt Regency Hotel downtown. One day, a friend of mine, who was working at American Airlines and who knew my husband, said to me, "Mamie, American is hiring, and you should think about applying. Your husband gets the hotel benefits, and if you work at American, you'll not only get hotel benefits but flight benefits as well! You guys could vacation anywhere!"

I thought, "What a deal!"

I applied and was hired by American Airlines as a reservation agent. This was attractive not only for the benefits, but it provided flexible hours. In the beginning, I worked the swing shift from 10:00

p.m. to 5:00 a.m. This allowed me to be with my children during the day, and I could work at night. Most days you could sign up for what American called "time leave," which allowed you to leave early or take whole days off at a time if they didn't need you. I took full advantage of the flexible hours and was able to manage home and work effectively without affecting my benefits. That way, I could be with my children. We were living in the hotel in Fort Worth on the top floor and had a housekeeper who could watch the children in the morning while I slept in, and then in the afternoon, the children had all my attention. It was the best of both worlds for me—I could be with my children, which was incredibly important, and be active in the workforce.

I was raised to set goals and have always been goal oriented. I loved helping to raise our children but knew I would always do something more. I didn't know exactly what that would be, but I was ready for anything. And then new opportunities arose.

It was 1987. My job at American was to take and build reservations over the phone. I got paid $5.75 an hour but had all the wonderful flight benefits. I was content at the time but was wondering what was next. I had been working the phones for about eighteen months (which can get tedious) when my supervisor tapped me on the shoulder.

"Hey, we have an opportunity for you to learn a new programming language for subject matter experts, such as yourself."

"What?" I replied. "Programming?"

"Yeah, it's what they call a fourth-generation programming language—4GL—a computer programming language that is intended to be easier for users than the older computer languages. Want to give it a shot?"

I was surprised at this.

"Why are you asking me?"

"Well," he replied, "we think that if *you* can do this, *anybody* can."

I laughed. I knew exactly what he meant—and I guess he meant it humorously. It meant that if *I* failed, then I am really stupid, because anybody should be able to do this thing!

Who could resist such an alluring challenge? I was, of course, intimidated by the offer, but being the competitive person that I am, I said yes and was determined not to fail. They paired me up with an industrial engineer, who was also a woman, and flew us to Australia for six weeks.

The technology that American Airlines used, and still uses today, is called Sabre. This system was first developed in the 1960s. It's what travel agents and other travel companies use all over the world—essentially the backbone of the searching, booking, and organizing of airlines, hotels, car rentals, tour operators, and the like. For six weeks we built the first user-friendly interface for booking flights that sat on top of the Sabre platform. This was my introduction to programming, and I really enjoyed it and found I also had an aptitude for it.

We rolled it out to American Airlines in the late 1980s, and it was a great success, so American began to market and sell it to other airlines, hotels, car rentals, rail systems, etc. It was one of the most successful revenue generators for Sabre and American at the time. What was key was the new technology could be built on top of older technology, and it was remarkably easy to do. You teach subject matter experts the fundamentals, they learn how to program, and they maintain it moving forward—then there is no need for ongoing consultants, which is how so much of the industry was working at the time.

I continued with this work for about six years, traveling all around the world. I ended up touching almost every aspect of the software business—design and development, sales, marketing, training, writing the curriculum for the training. Our product, called QIK, is still used today on the Sabre system and has been in its portfolio since its launch.

Meanwhile, my three children were starting school, and I was doing the usual thing that keeps moms busy—kids' sports, music, you name it. It became impossible for me to continue traveling the world, and I just didn't want to sacrifice so much of my family time. But I was building a career and wanted to continue my growth. I knew I had to do something different that kept me off the road.

I was given three choices. I could stay doing what I was doing, or I could pursue work in the pricing and yield management team. Or, they said, there's "this thing" called "the internet" where there was a keen focus on launching online travel booking capabilities.

"If you don't want to travel, you might want to check out this internet option," they said. And that is exactly what I did.

It was 1995, and I was in my early thirties. While computers were certainly much more mainstream than in the eighties, and Microsoft, in particular, pushed the PC into the public limelight with the launch of Windows 95 (complete with a Rolling Stones marketing stunt with the song "Start Me Up"), computers weren't as ubiquitous as they are today. So, I took up the offer but knew I was throwing myself into the deep end in more ways than one.

Sabre decided to bring me on board in its operations research group, which at the time led the QIK development. This was not the norm. In the group, they only hired computer science experts and industrial engineers, but because I was a subject matter expert (SME) on Sabre, knew the QIK programming language, and held a master's degree, they agreed to bring me on board. I was told later that without the master's degree, I would not have been hired. I never would have guessed when I was studying that this would be the direction and the doors my master's degree would open for me. I've always thought my dad's advice about preparing yourself for serendipitous opportunities was absolutely right, and I have followed it ever since.

When I joined Sabre, my boss was the original industrial engineer I was paired with in Australia. Despite my lack of experience in engineering or computer science, I was training all the new hires because of my education background. These were all industrial engineers, especially in the first eighteen-month period. We were trying to hire as many as we could to build off the success of the platform and grow opportunities.

As the product and program grew over the next couple of years, I began to notice a trend. All the people who were brought on after me—who I helped hire and train as the new hires—were getting promoted. But I was still in the same position. I kept telling myself that it was OK, that I shouldn't worry, and that I could trust the people I was working with to do the right thing.

Well into my third year, the last person we hired in the team was promoted. I simply didn't understand why everyone was promoted except me, and I was incredibly frustrated. I finally worked up the courage to call a meeting with my bosses (both women) to have them explain why everyone else was being promoted. I presented my contributions, outcomes, and successes and asked them flat out what was going on with my opportunities.

They said, "We thought you wanted to focus more on your family. We didn't think you wanted to be promoted."

I was shocked and extremely disappointed at this reply.

I made it immediately clear that this was not the case and that I was disappointed that they made this assumption and subsequent decisions without ever discussing the matter with me. Why not just ask? Why not just talk? I told them I was not only concerned about the way this was being handled and the assumptions made, but that this was, in fact, discriminatory.

Since then, I have shared this lesson with many men and women: you must manage your own career. You need to trust your colleagues and leaders if you're to have a healthy working environment, but you also need to verify information and have critical career discussions frequently so that others understand your aspirations and what motivates you. In my case, I really thought that since my bosses were women, they were going to speak for me and help develop my career. I assumed that they would think I had the same motivations and aspirations as they did, but it turned out this wasn't the case. While I think what they did was wrong, the fact of the matter is I didn't make myself clear either. This was a rude awakening for me to realize that I play a part in making my career happen. I was waiting for somebody to do something for me and wasn't managing it for myself, when from the beginning, I should have made my expectations clear. Have the courage to talk about what you want and be clear and open about where you want to go in your career.

From my courageous career discussion with my bosses, they realized immediately they made a huge mistake and finally promoted me and beefed up my salary as much as they could to close the gap with other engineers' salaries. But it did take me longer—especially given the fact that I had joined American making $5.75 an hour and then, even converting to the Sabre group, was still not making anything near to what others were making at the time. Again, another good lesson learned.

So much of building a good career, and leading people through transformation, is about communicating. When it comes to your own transformation, you need to also learn to ask for help. Asking for help is not a weakness. In fact, it's a strength, and I've seen this repeatedly.

In my work environment in Sabre, everyone was an engineering expert except myself. I was programming, which I enjoyed, but I had very little exposure to computers or any of the computer applications when I joined. I remember vividly the day when I was asked to prepare a presentation on our progress for our executives. I was petrified, and there was no way around it. I didn't know the applications we were using. I didn't know how to navigate Microsoft applications and had to prepare my presentation in Microsoft PowerPoint, which I was unfamiliar with. (Remember, it was the early nineties!) I just didn't have the experience and was terrified that everyone would think I was stupid and would say, "Who the heck did they just hire for this job?" So much was going through my mind at the time.

I *had* to ask for help.

I thought carefully about how I would do this. There was one guy in the office who I thought, "He seems like a nice guy; I'll ask him for help."

So I sat him down and simply said, "Can you help me here? I have a couple of questions."

It was such a good learning experience. Not only did he help me with the questions I had, but he went out of his way to go even further. "Take a look at all these other cool things you can do!" he said, showing me around. He was so willing to help—excited at the prospect, in fact.

Most people are willing to help, believe me. Moreover, he invited me to ask for additional help, anytime. And I did take him up on that in those early days.

I joined Travelocity in the fall of 1995, and we launched the first travel website, Travelocity.com, in March of 1996. It completely revolutionized the travel industry, and I was privileged to be in the center of it as the senior director of development. It was a wild ride for three years—I remember having constant application volume issues over Christmas because systems would continually crash with the extraordinary number of users. We had to constantly upgrade our system hardware to manage the exponential volume growth. Every October, every January, the systems would crater because the volumes were so far above anything we could have predicted. This is when I learned how to build resilient applications.

I had to learn to lead by example, to do what everyone else was being asked to do during these challenging times. I had to sacrifice time with my family to meet the needs of the business. This was difficult, but we had millions of customers counting on us. I learned that I never wanted to be in scramble mode again. I learned a lot from these early years and carried much of those lessons into my subsequent positions.

And it's where I learned that it wasn't actually about me. Shortly after getting that book by Stephen Covey anonymously dropped on my desk, Sabre offered a leadership training course through the University of Virginia, Darden School of Business, and it was in that course I was to receive a massive eye-opener. The course was based on the brilliant material from James Kouzes and Barry Z. Posner, *The Leadership Challenge*. Jack and Carol Weber, an absolute power couple in executive and strategic change management, taught the course. Both have created numerous and highly innovative executive development programs, rated by *Financial Times* and the *Wall Street Journal* as among the best senior management programs globally. It was a wonderful privilege to attend this prestigious training.

To this day I still advise everyone to get what they can of the Webers' research (there's plenty to find on the internet) and get a copy of *The Leadership Challenge*. I was absolutely mesmerized by the remarkably simple, yet effective, approach. I was honored when I got selected at Sabre to be one of the ten "train the trainers," and we worked with Jack and Carol for a week, who taught us how to teach the material.

When you attend the course, as part of the training, you are required to complete a survey, answering questions about yourself. You then select twelve peers and subordinates, and each person anonymously takes the survey and answers the same questions about you. You match what others think about you versus what you think about yourself. The survey was focused on the five practices detailed in *The Leadership Challenge* (Model the Way, Inspire a Shared Vision, Challenge the Process, Enable Others to Act, and Encourage the Heart).[4] You answer several questions under each of these practices, and then the answers are summarized in a succinct report.

What a rude awakening and enormous learning this was for me! All my personal scores about myself basically said two words: "I'm great!" Everyone else's scores basically said two very different words about me: "You are not great!" I did not inspire people with a shared vision, I did more of "do as I say, not as I do" behavior. I overreacted to challenges instead of enabling my team to react. And I didn't reward and recognize great work.

I went to bed that night embarrassed and perplexed, and I agonized over that for a very long time. When I attended the Darden training course with Jack and Carol, it was my turning point in my journey to building true self-awareness. I needed to change my entire outlook, my entire approach—and find new motivation—because what I was doing was not working.

I realized that the people around me needed to be my motivation. It's not all about you. If you galvanize a team around a compelling goal,

---

4   J. M. Kouzes and B. Z. Posner, *The Leadership Challenge: How to Make Extraordinary Things Happen in Organizations* (New York, NY: John Wiley & Sons, 2023).

if you motivate them to do their best, if you recognize all their efforts, big and small, your chances of success are greater. But if you chase success just for yourself, everyone will have two words for you: *you suck*.

Since those early days, as I've led numerous large corporations through significant transformations, I've always wanted to thank the person who left that book on my desk. I owe them a lot of gratitude as it set the tone for my career and my leadership development journey.

I was at American/Sabre/Travelocity.com for twenty years from 1987 to 2007. In my first three years, I served as the reservation agent at American Airlines, and Sabre was a part of American. From 1989 to 1995, I served as a programmer helping to build the numerous QIK applications under the Sabre umbrella. Sabre and American split in June of 1996. I then served as the senior director of development for Travelocity (1995 to 1998). I was responsible for all application development and in charge of preparing and presenting all design, development, and implementation proposals. I grew the development team from 45 to approximately 150 developers while managing a $30 million budget. I also implemented the company's first content management system, as well as its data warehouse on the Teradata platform.

In addition, I implemented online personalization and delivered improved reporting and insight capabilities from a twenty-four-hour cycle to less than one hour, which increased revenue by more than 30 percent. I reduced employee attrition from 51 percent in those early internet days to 7 percent by developing a performance management system to reward and recognize exceptional talent; and I developed a grassroots leadership program across the Sabre organization designed to promote leadership at all levels. Transformation only happens when everyone is engaged—and it's up to you to lead them there!

In 1998, I was promoted to senior vice president and led all aspects of product development at Travelocity.com. I grew and led a technical team of more than five hundred professionals globally. I helped create and implement the Travelocity and Sabre global sourcing strategy and road map to consolidate development offices, reduce offshore vendors, and standardize global infrastructure. In the first year, Sabre realized savings of $9 million, representing a 5 percent improvement in operating expenses.

Alongside the team I was leading, I transformed Travelocity and Sabre's software development practices, replacing Waterfall methods with Agile development, and improving the speed to market by 30 to 40 percent. I believe Agile is part of the reason we scored so well in the annual employee engagement survey. Additionally, product quality was improved with a reduction in defects of more than 30 percent.

During all that time and in these various positions, I kept noticing how people worked through change, transition, and transformation—and how that changed an organization. I ended my tenure at Travelocity in April 2007 and joined the Dell team for a year, and then Dun & Bradstreet from 2008 to 2011. It was when I joined Intuit in September 2011 that I was able to codify and implement my playbook that others can employ today.

This book is the outcome of not only my personal journey, which I hope inspires you and gets you motivated, but also the playbook in its entirety. I'm not just going to talk about what you can do but also convey to you *how* to do it. It won't be a book to read and put on the shelf, but one you can come back to and work through as you implement various stages of your transformation efforts—taking your people, your organization, and your company to new heights.

My playbook for transformational change consists of six stages. The graphic below illustrates how each of these works together.

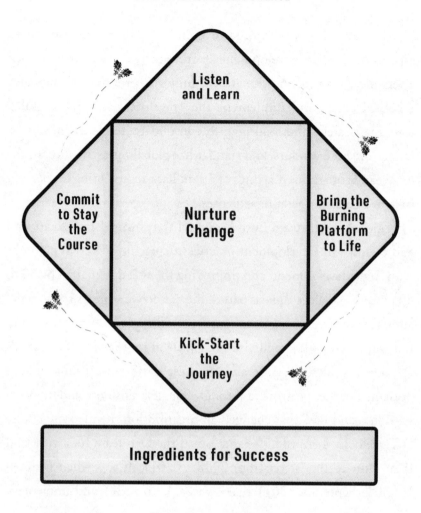

Each chapter in this book will follow the playbook in order:

Chapter 1: Ingredients for Success (The Foundation for Transformation)

Chapter 2: Listen and Learn (Create the Right Environment)

Chapter 3: Bring the Burning Platform to Life (Capture Hearts and Minds)

Chapter 4: Kick-start the Journey

Chapter 5: Commit to Stay the Course

Chapter 6: Nurture Change

The arrows on the outside of the diagram represent the cyclic nature of transformation, with nurturing change at the heart and center of the playbook. Transformation is a perpetual process and nurturing change will be a consistent theme.

I suggest, before you begin to unpack this process, that you carefully consider your own motivations, ambitions, and methods. You have to decide: Do you have the courage and what it takes to drive difficult change? Are you able to establish a compelling enough vision for those you now lead? You must first grasp the fact that it's not all about you but about the people *you serve*.

If I've piqued your interest, I would like to invite you to take action. It's time to lead your organization through extraordinary change! And remember, this is an *ongoing* process. It's never once and done. But you need to start, and that time is now!

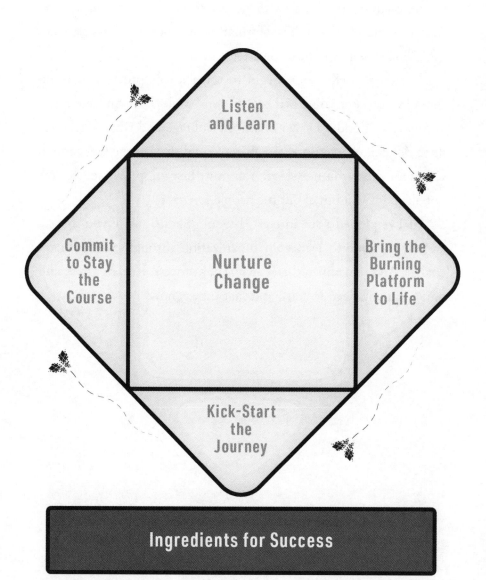

Ingredients for Success

CHAPTER 1

Ingredients for Success

*Leadership is the lifting of a person's vision to higher sights,
the raising of a person's performance to a higher standard, the
building of a person's personality beyond its normal limitations.*

—PETER DRUCKER

The Foundation for Transformation

What drives the need for transformational change in an organization? Usually it's because the company, business unit, or team is not performing against the organization's vision or strategic goals. It often faces competitive threats, industry disruptions, or other organizational challenges. When a company faces the need for extraordinary change, the organization's leadership looks for people who can come in and alter the trajectory of the current state.

If this describes what you are facing, then you need to start by assessing if you're in a position to drive the change. Throughout my career, I have seen many examples of companies that want to change but do not provide the right *ingredients for success*. They don't realize that things like sponsorship, support, and providing autonomy are essential for any successful transformation effort. Transformation is easy to talk about, but it is difficult to do. Talk is cheap when you're being asked to take big risks and swings that others may not be willing to do themselves.

To be successful, you must evaluate your current work environment and the leadership willingness and capability to support change. This is the foundation of any transformation effort, and if this foundation is not in place, your efforts may be jeopardized. If you have the right ingredients in place, or a reasonable majority, then your chances of success are much more favorable.

What fits your situation?

A. You've been asked to join a new company that wants you to lead or help drive transformation.

B. You've recently joined a company that's asked you to lead or help drive transformation.

C. You've been working in a company for a while and have been asked to lead or drive transformation.

Whether you are (A), (B), or (C), you might not realize that you *can* assess the environment you are working in or are about to join and determine if you're in the right position to be successful in the difficult journey of transformation. Many people in (C) might think they know the environment, but they will need to follow the same process I'm proposing, as there are many aspects that will surprise you in conducting your evaluation.

By the end of this chapter, you will have the right tools to evaluate your environment to determine if the right ingredients exist to undertake the transformation journey, and what your chances are for success.

Fight for Autonomy

Travelocity—a combination of the two words "travel" and "velocity," pointing to speed in booking travel—originally spun out of Sabre in the mid-'90s. We were the first mover in the online travel space, and if I recall, the only online company from a major corporation that survived the dot-com crash in the early 2000s. I was one of the first ten employees of Travelocity and was there from the beginning in 1995, seeing the launch in March of 1996.

When I first came into Travelocity, we were small and nimble and able to move quickly, but over several years, as the teams grew and more coordination was needed across Sabre and Travelocity, our processes started getting bloated with lots of corporate oversight. More time was being spent on inspection of the project plan rather than on speed of design, development, and delivery. The process of how we developed our software was creating conflict that needed to be resolved. We were agonizing over project requirements that would go back and forth between teams, creating ill will. It was taking too long to solidify requirements, and by the time the software was built, tested, and released, the product managers would inform the development team that it wasn't what they originally wanted, and it wasn't delivering the customer benefit. Finger-pointing then became the norm. This frustrated everyone and created more tension between teams, and things only got more stressed as releases rolled out late and there were too many errors. Relationships continued to deteriorate, and animosity escalated across teams.

At the time we were using a Waterfall methodology to develop our software. This consists of several phases to be followed linearly, meaning one phase can't start until the previous is completed. Using this process, you typically have a product manager who gathers data and customer requirements, and then comes up with the idea of what they want built. The product manager creates an extensive set of requirements, which at the time we called "the brick." The detailed requirements have *everything* the product team wants, from look and feel, features and functionality, application flow, etc. When completed, this gets handed over to the development team who must build the software. We called this "throwing the brick over the fence" to the development team. This team must then interpret the requirements (often misunderstood), and then translate this to the necessary teams for development. It was an arduous process.

The problem was the development process could take months before it was finished, depending on how extensive the original requirements were. In one case, it took us as much as a year to develop a major innovation, which was followed by extensive testing. Once ready for testing, the product team gets its first peek at the product and features and are able to provide feedback.

You can probably see how this creates dilemmas in a software development scenario. Once the product manager gets to tinker with the application, they are immediately saying things like, "This isn't what I meant," or "This isn't what the customer wants." After a year of development, it stands to reason that the customer's wants and needs would have changed. The requirements set out a year ago or even a few months ago are no longer useful or relevant.

We started looking at each other as enemies; development teams versus product teams. It was such an unhealthy and unproductive way to operate, especially in the ever-growing, competitive internet travel environment. Yet this was how we were all behaving because we were frustrated with the process and felt paralyzed. It was taking all the fun out of what we were doing. I loved our work, and we were at the forefront of internet development. I loved the people I was working with every day. So it seemed to me that the issue wasn't really the people or even our abilities; it was our process.

Changing Process

I thought there must be a better way to develop software, so I began researching alternatives. I heard of one particular gentleman in another Sabre organization who was using Extreme Programming (XP). I met with him, and he showed me what they were doing, and I was blown away by the simplicity of the approach, the quality they were producing, and the dramatic results they were achieving. They completely flipped the development approach we were trained in, and instead of linear development moved to an Agile, flexible methodology.

If you're unfamiliar with the concept, here's how XP works. The entire team, from product to technology, is located together. The project is broken into manageable chunks of work that can be designed, developed, and tested in what we call short sprints, usually two weeks in length. Requirements, design, development, and testing are all done together with the entire team. Engineers are paired to develop the features with each other, and at the end of the sprint, you release working software to customers. You then get immediate feedback and are able to quickly adjust requirements based on the customers' feedback, rather than waiting months.

This was the first time I was introduced to an Agile methodology. I saw at once that we could launch product features in shorter chunks for the benefit of our customers. Today, this methodology is practiced in many different industries, but in the early 2000s, it was a new idea and pushed the envelope of what leaders and developers were used to.

We needed to infuse new change in our environment, and I wanted to give this a try. I could see the success the other team was having, and I wanted to replicate their success. While I didn't know if this approach was guaranteed to work, I knew we had to take a swing and do something different. My plan was to use the scrum methodology, very similar to XP, but (unlike XP) I didn't have the luxury of being able to have two engineers sitting together working the same piece of code.

I approached my boss, the CEO, to share this new methodology and request support to pursue this new approach. The answer was "not interested." The general sentiment was "don't rock the boat." Waterfall methodology was tried and tested and used in other reputable industries, so it should serve us well, and we needed to just do it better. I left the meeting disappointed yet not surprised.

Since I'm not one to take no for an answer, I told myself, "I'm going to do it, and I'm going to ask for forgiveness, not permission."

This has been a common motto of mine throughout my career, and it's one I really advise people to follow. Sometimes it's necessary to ask forgiveness rather than permission. People need to see something in action and understand the results for themselves. Remember, most people resist change, and not everyone can see the potential of something new until they see it work with concrete results. I knew it was going to be controversial, but I also knew the tremendous possibilities waiting for us if we gave this new approach a chance.

Courage to Rock the Boat

I went to my team and simply asked them, "Who wants to volunteer for an experiment?" Asking people versus telling people to volunteer (this is being "voluntold"!) is a powerful method. I was surprised by the number of people who were willing to take the swing with me. With the team in place, I hired a consulting firm to train us in scrum and coach us through our experiment. (Remember, asking for help is not a weakness!) I also found a willing product manager who would work with the new team. Doing it this way would give me much more leverage with the skeptics on our executive team.

With everything set, the consulting firm came in, and we picked a project together. We later realized it was the wrong project, as it was simply too big and too important. You should normally pick a smaller project that you can cut your teeth on and ensure a higher degree of success. This increased the pressure on the team, having so much at stake. But nevertheless, it ended up being incredibly successful. The project was delivered ahead of schedule with a high degree of quality, two factors that didn't often come together in our development environment! This triumph resulted in more buy-in with leadership and the broader teams. They simply loved the process and, more importantly, the speed at which we delivered the bottom-line results for the company and the outcomes for our customers.

This quote from Margaret Mead has always stuck with me, and I've shared it with teams that are embarking on significant change:

> *Never doubt that a small group of thoughtful, committed citizens can change the world. Indeed, it is the only thing that ever has.*
> —MARGARET MEAD

The Flywheel Effect

As a result of these early successes, the more work we did in this manner, the greater momentum we gained. The success we achieved as a team further encouraged us, and everyone was sensing the positive change in the environment. Eventually our work was just better, the results for customers were superior, and impacts on the bottom line were increasing. When a team delivers exceptional results, recognition follows, and people start to stand up and take notice.

Engineers just want to build something great—and to see it *used*. And, like all of us, they want to do it in a way where they are valued and recognized. After all our success, we kept hearing other teams saying they wanted to try this new method as well, and they were going to move in the same direction. It was changing the culture of the company. This is what we call the flywheel effect. You start small, and as you move forward, you gain momentum. After several years, the entire Sabre organization adopted Agile methodologies due to multiple teams' proven successes and our collective willingness to experiment and try something new.

None of the changes I implemented, and the changes that came as a result, would have been possible if certain ingredients within the environment were not there. In the years that followed and as I led other companies through transformation efforts, the same patterns kept repeating. That is when I realized that when the right ingredients for success exist in your environment, you are in a position to drive fundamental change.

Intuit—Looking for the Right Ingredients

Intuit's ProTax group needed significant change in its online capabilities. The company was trying to launch an effective online professional tax application for four years but was not having success. They needed someone to come in and lead extraordinary change because there was a big risk Intuit would fall behind the industry momentum to move online.

Before I joined Intuit, I worked for a company where, after a short period of time, I realized I made a very poor employer choice. This happened because I didn't do my homework before joining. I didn't ask the right questions and didn't probe for the right ingredients. The leaders were set in their ways and were not ethical, and decisions were all top-down. Transformation was not desired, even when it was obviously needed. I didn't flesh out the factors that I began to realize were imperative for transformational success. I learned so much from that experience and decided there was no way that was ever going to happen to me again.

This initiated a different approach when I was asked to interview with Intuit. By the end of the process, I had eighteen interviews with a myriad of leaders across the company, including the CEO. While Intuit's leaders were assessing me, I was also assessing them. I wanted to be completely sure that the ingredients I was looking for were present in the company.

After all the interviews were done, I requested another meeting with the general manager (GM) so that I could ask some additional questions to ensure the ingredients I was seeking were in place. My overall question in this process was simple: *Someone is asking me to lead extraordinary change. But am I being set up for success? Or failure?*

Would I have autonomy? Would I have decision-making authority? Would the GM have my back when we faced adversity? These were the kind of questions I ended up asking. Based on my assessment after all these interviews, I felt extremely positive about joining Intuit. After four months, I was offered the position of vice president (VP) of product development for Intuit's Professional Tax Group. I went in with eyes wide open, knowing most of the ingredients for success were present in the organization, and I accepted this position with enthusiasm.

Now, I'm happy to say, Intuit does not do this extensive interview process any longer but has implemented a new and improved Agile approach to hiring, which has been extremely effective.

Serving Intuit

It was a pleasure and honor to serve at Intuit for nine years, successfully leading transformation through talent, process, and platform upgrades. I was promoted to senior VP and given additional teams and new responsibilities as a result of delivering game-changing results. We consistently delivered new online capabilities while also transforming our legacy desktop products. We gave autonomy to teams so they could think differently and innovate in ways they never dreamed of before. We transformed our development processes from Waterfall to Agile (scrum) and delivered several firsts for Intuit. I left the company proud of the incredible achievements we delivered as a team.

The bottom line is this: when the right ingredients exist, you have the opportunity to create your work environment and culture. This is sometimes difficult to believe, but it's absolutely true and achievable. Believe me, if I can do it, so can you.

There are several ingredients for success, and while each one is important, they may not all be present in your environment. However, a good portion should be present to varying degrees. Let's look at the ingredients.

The Ingredients

1. Support

You obviously won't have everyone's support, but you do need to have the *right* support. Here are questions you can ask under this heading:

A. Do You/Will You Have a Boss You Can Count On?

Make sure they will provide a safety net. It's not just up to you to take risks but for risks to be taken *together*. Sometimes the leaders of an organization are looking for a "fall guy" to make all the tough decisions as they may want to distance themselves from risk. Are they there for you or just looking for someone to take the blame when the going gets tough? You need to ask situational questions around having autonomy so you can assess their commitment. Questions with *Yes* and *No* answers do not work.

An example question: "I'm going to change how we develop our software, and I am going to begin this transition next week—and it may ruffle some feathers across the company. Will you support my decision to make this change even if you receive negative feedback?"

B. Will They Support You through Tough Decisions?

It's easy to support you in the obvious decisions, but what about tough decisions, like losing a valuable skilled employee because they are unwilling or unable to get on board? Will your leadership support you in this type of scenario? Or will they hesitate and allow their own fear or self-preservation to get in the way?

An example question: "I need to take action on an employee for poor work performance. I know you value this employee, but will you support my decision to move forward even if it makes you and HR uncomfortable?"

C. Will They Allow You to Move Quickly?

I've often been called a bull in a china shop, but transformation can sound good in theory and yet can be very uncomfortable to put into practice. Old ways of working are going to need to break! As you kick -start your bold journey, some will accuse you of being that bull. You are doing exactly what they have asked you to do, but when the rubber meets the road, some may hesitate. You need to be able to move quickly rather than be pulled into endless meetings to explain your rationale.

An example question: "I'm restructuring my organization, and I'm going to start the communication and change management process in two days. Do I have your support to begin this change?

2. Autonomy

There is nothing more important than having autonomy. The opposite of autonomy is micromanagement. If you are being asked to take on a significant task, fraught with risk, you need to know whether you have the right kind of independence to make the required important-but-tough decisions. You should not have to jump through hoops when you are trying to move forward with speed. You need to be able to spend money reasonably where needed and cut where necessary. You need to be able to change your team when required. Even your superiors need to get comfortable with the fact that you might move their "friends/allies" to different teams—or move them out altogether.

As I unpack the playbook, you will note that many of its stages will require you to have autonomy. It's not enough to just be told, "Yes, you will have autonomy." You need to ask some detailed questions to determine your level of autonomy. Some of these could be: "Will you push back or allow me to do what I feel is necessary?" or, "Are you ready to accept my assessment of talent?" This is a discussion that needs to happen before embarking on change, so you know what you're up against.

If your discussions cannot be candid, that in itself is an answer to your questions.

3. Meritocracy or Biased Performance Management

Does your organization recognize employees based on their demonstrated abilities and merit? You will be surprised to discover that many companies don't take the time to formulate concrete, measurable goals. In a meritocracy, this is imperative. Without concrete goals, the wrong people will be rewarded or promoted—and often not based on their achievements. This creates a negative culture that employees will despise. When you effectively set goals and reward the right outcomes, you find employees will be motivated to go beyond what you imagined. But you must monitor, measure, and coach frequently and consistently to ensure the meritocracy remains healthy.

Implementing an effective performance management system will help to accelerate your change efforts. It requires documenting the current state, setting lofty goals, and measuring against the goals frequently and consistently.

There are two sets of employee goals: organizational goals and developmental goals. While both are important, developmental goals are a higher priority to me because when you get the right people with the right attitude and skill on board, and reward them for their results and positive behaviors, the company goals are better realized. Just going after the company goals without evaluating the talent will be a much bigger struggle.

Here are a few key questions you can use to probe for further understanding:

"Is the company setting lofty goals against a compelling vision, and if so, what are these goals?"

"What grand challenges are being set?"

"How is the company making time for employees to think about achieving things they haven't thought possible before?"

Are leaders willing to admit they don't have the right people, and know how to address it?"

"How is employee performance measured?"

4. Compelling Vision

Everyone hates empty slogans, and for good reason, but having a great, compelling vision is imperative. Otherwise, people will just continue doing what they've always done, which of course limits what you can achieve. There is a wonderful saying that I use frequently: "The thinking that got us here won't get us out."

The company might be bringing you in to help formulate a compelling vision, but remember it is important to set the right tone early. You need to have a vision that is a declaration, aspirational, easy to understand, and simple to remember. It is one you constantly communicate and revisit as your organization evolves. The vision is the "True North" of where the organization is going and guides the strategy.

Is there a common language at the leadership level and across the company? This is not a question to ask in discussions or interviews, but it is one you can observe for yourself. When I went through my round of interviews at Intuit, I began to notice how each member of the leadership team used nearly identical language. That was a good sign. A common language means a common vision exists—and if this language is consistent even across different branches, offices, or a mobile work team, that's a great sign of a great culture and environment. It's something that cannot be faked.

As you begin any transformation effort, if there is no common vision and inconsistent messaging, you will have a harder time getting teams aligned on the change that is needed. Make it a top priority to establish a compelling vision and align on the consistent messaging. Once established, include this in the development goals of your managers and key individual contributors.

In their research compiled into the book *The Technology Fallacy*, Gerald C. Kane et al. speak of four skills that are critical in transformation: "Transformative Vision," a "Forward-Looking Perspective," an "Understanding of Technology," and "Change Orientation."[5] In

---

5   G. C. Kane, A. N. Phillips, J. R. Copulsky, and G. R. Andrus, *The Technology Fallacy: How People Are the Real Key to Digital Transformation* (MIT Press, 2019).

my estimation, if you have the first of these—the transformative vision—the rest will take care of themselves. To further bolster this observation, in Jim Kouzes and Barry Posner's classic book, *The Leadership Challenge*, they collected stories from thousands of people to understand what effective leaders do when they are being their best, and one aspect that was crucial in all these stories was the importance of a shared vision. This shows how imperative an inspiring vision is and how critical it is, regardless of your industry.

By setting a compelling vision and lofty goals, people will rise to the occasion. When done right, it is exciting to watch people react, and it's fun to be a part of the process.

5. HR Support

You will step on toes when it comes to making people decisions. Some employees will leave voluntarily while others will leave involuntarily. The question here is whether HR is ready to support you in making tough people decisions. Will they support you or work against you, especially as things get more difficult? Or when a highly skilled but negative (in behavior) employee leaves? Will they trust you with knowing which talent and skill is best for the job? Will they support the people you've decided to bring on board? Will they support changes in hiring processes? Will they try to dissuade you from making organizational changes? There are many questions you can ask, but you need to probe deeply into this area.

6. Data or Supposition?

When "I think," "I feel," and "I believe" phrases are being used to make decisions, it is a bad sign. Just because someone feels a certain way does not make it so. This is where you need to look at whether your organization is making decisions based on facts or feelings. Look for the phrases, "I know … I have demonstrated … I have proved," which show that data is being used to promote effective decision-making.

An example question: "Give me an example of how the organization determines the portfolio, development, and feature priorities. What data is used to make these important decisions?"

An Assessment Tool

At my website, mamiefjones.com, I provide a detailed assessment tool that will assist you in measuring which of the ingredients can be found in your organization, and to what degree. A high score will, of course, offer a greater chance of success. However, if you score high in some areas and low in others, you can still achieve success, but it may require a bit more courage and risk-taking to effect the needed change. If you have lower scores across the board, your chances for success will be lower. Based on your score, you can make a decision on how willing you are to take up the challenge.

Whether you are joining a company or are already in place, this is a decision point that should be thought through carefully. Move forward, or move on?

To access the assessment tool, scan the QR code below.

Scan this QR code to access an assessment tool to measure how your environment is ready for change.

Other Essentials

Once you have assessed your environment for the ingredients for success, there are other important elements that you will need to focus your attention on. Some elements will require heavy lifting in the early stages of your transformation effort, and others will require your courage and tenacity to maintain. Let's look at these essentials.

1. Identify Great Talent

Realize that there are exceptional people in the organization. They were great once, and they can be great again. In my case at Travelocity, my team had achieved greatness in our early years, and so I knew we could do it again. We had the talent, but what was bringing us down was the *process*. By setting the right vision and goals, the great talent will step up to the challenge. It's your responsibility to inspire, motivate, coach, and ultimately give people the autonomy they need once they have proved themselves capable.

2. Identify Change Agents

Recognize early that there are those in the organization that feel stuck and are hungry to do amazing work, but the culture and the environment are in their way. As you evaluate your team, you will have to start identifying those individuals, as they will rise to the occasion with you to take risks and big swings.

In my experience at Travelocity, once we identified a few brave souls that were willing to experiment with scrum, they were able to influence others through the success we achieved. I have found this same pattern in every organization I've taken through transformation. These are self-motivated people who are ready to do something different, be it from frustration or natural curiosity and creativity.

They help to create the flywheel effect. In the next chapter, I will show you how to find them.

3. Make a Statement Early

Once you decide to embark on this journey, it is incredibly important to set high expectations early by conveying the vision and communicating lofty goals. You must make it very clear that everyone will be required to meet the new expectations. There will be those that will not want to get on board, and it's pretty clear early on who these people are. Your work will be to inspire your team members to join in the transformation effort. Most people will rise to the occasion as they see this as an opportunity to do something great for customers and expand their skills to grow in their career. However, there will be some who will not manage the transition well, and you will need to help them seek opportunities elsewhere. If they linger in the team, even if they are highly skilled, they will sabotage your efforts and create a toxic environment.

When you have employees with this mindset, you need to take action and remove them from the team. This is "the statement" you need to make early, and when you do, it does three things:

1. It convinces the other employees to take action who may be on the fence about their position. They will assess their outlook and decide to stay or find other opportunities for themselves.

2. When a toxic employee leaves the team, it lifts up the others who are eager to change but have been held back by a limiting culture. They will be grateful for your early action and consistency, and inspired to help accelerate the new direction.

3. It opens the door to bring in exceptional new talent and gives momentum to building flywheel effect.

This is the hardest thing you will do, but it is one of the most important actions you must take. It sets the tone for the organization moving forward. In the chapters that follow, I will unpack how you can inspire and motivate people toward change, and how you can help those who are not a good fit to find new opportunities.

4. Expect Resistance

Jack Welsh, former CEO of General Electric, wrote the book, *Straight from the Gut*, in which he outlines how many exceptional individuals committed to a cause long ago struggle later when the world or the environment has changed.[6] People will resist the transformation you are bringing because it will be very difficult for them to accept that change is inevitable. Not everyone in the organization is wired to succeed in a changing environment, and you will need to really help people work through the emotions and realities that they will experience.

You have to give everyone multiple opportunities to get on board, but some will resist the change no matter how hard you work to get them engaged.

You should also expect some resistance from other executives who are not entirely sure why so much needs to change, and so quickly. As you begin to deliver early wins, you will build trust with those that may have been skeptical in the beginning.

5. Document Current State and Demonstrate Small Wins Early

In order to prove that you are making progress, it is crucial to document your current state. By documenting your current state, it serves as a baseline to begin measurement against goals. As teams start to show early wins, you communicate this broadly across the

---

6   J. Welch and J. A. Byrne, *Jack: Straight from the Gut* (New York, NY: Business Plus, 2003).

organization and recognize those individuals and teams publicly that are making the effort. This does two things:

1. It begins to form a sentiment across the organization that you know what you're doing because you are delivering concrete results. People can't argue with results.

2. It helps to boost morale among your teams because they will realize you care about the work they do and that more recognition will follow.

I can't emphasize enough that data will furnish the speed at which you move and provide the ammunition to prove your progress. As trust continues to grow, the flywheel gains momentum. Don't be afraid to showcase the teams' successes—it inspires people to do more!

Here are a few categories that you can begin to capture as you begin to document your current state. While some of these are focused on technology, you will find your own areas to improve. The important thing to remember is if you have identified any challenge, capture the current state so you can set the appropriate goals and report on all areas of improvement.

1. **People**—Document existing skills and behaviors, which will help you begin to craft new talent goals and expectations. As new talent joins and the makeup of the team changes, report your progress, improved speed of development, etc.

2. **Process**—Document gaps or failures in processes. As you close gaps, adopt new tools, etc., report on all concrete improvements.

3. **Platform**—Capture technology, architecture, application, and system performance metrics. This is a common measurement in most companies, and you will be asked to provide reports on improved performance, cost savings, etc.

4. **Organizational challenges**—you will find themes that will help you craft the needed organizational changes. Are people sitting together? Is there animosity across organizations? Is there effective resource utilization? There are many aspects of organizational challenges that you need to document and address over time.

How do you understand the true current state? This will all become quite clear in the next phase of the playbook, "Listen and Learn." Once you have your current state documented (which we will discuss in more detail in the next chapter), you must use data to measure your progress against each and every goal. As you show progress, it will begin to build trust across the organization and propel the flywheel.

6. Be Persistent

It's going to be a wild ride! Remember, it's not easy—nothing great is easily won! Keep on going! Change is the only constant, yet it is the one thing that human beings fight because we find security in our routines. We are all creatures of habit. For this reason, you will get pushback. Try not to take it personally. People are responding to their own fears and insecurities. While some will have the courage to voice their displeasure to you privately and publicly, there will be others who may take a more passive-aggressive approach. Those who are on board and those who are skeptical will need to understand that there is tremendous opportunity for them if they embrace what is happening. Helping people through this process is going to be the hardest challenge you will face, and it takes incredible persistence to stay the course. When you do, the team will be grateful for your leadership, and it will continue to lift the team to new heights.

I have developed a script I follow that helps me quickly discover employee mindsets and who are the emerging change agents. You also start to identify potential saboteurs—people who can short-circuit the process, not always maliciously but because of their own challenges and situations. It comes down to engaging people and simply asking probing questions. In the next chapter, I will introduce you to this script.

Your Readiness

While assessing your environment is absolutely key, you need also to assess your own readiness. Do you have the courage to step up and put yourself out there? Are you ready to take risks to drive change? Can you be persistent through all the ups and downs that come with leading extraordinary change?

To drive this type of effort, you must possess a keen sense of self-awareness. Understanding your strengths and weaknesses is important. You will need to lean on others to help you in your areas of opportunity. You cannot do this alone and will need to know when to ask for help. Remember, asking for help is not a weakness!

Your courage to drive change can influence your degree of success. Maybe your environment does not seem quite ready on the assessment tool score, but with the right mindset, self-awareness, and courage you can decide whether or not to take the swing. At Travelocity, I knew we needed to change. I didn't have all the ingredients in place, but I had some incredible people who also wanted to take a risk with me. Now is your time—are you ready to meet the challenge?

Time to Rise Up and Activate the Playbook

Now that you have decided to pursue this transformation, and you've calculated how many of the ingredients are in place, which is the foundation you need, you are ready to engage your team and the organization. Here is how the rest of the playbook will unfold in this book:

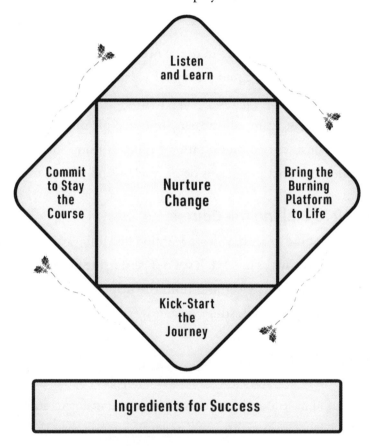

Listen and Learn: Creating the Right Environment

In this part of the process, you will be assessing the current state of your organization through an extensive listening and learning process. Be ready for many conversations. In the next chapter, I will provide a script you can follow and a guide on what to do. Only once you know the current state can you know what to do moving forward.

Bring the Burning Platform to Life: Capture Hearts and Minds

Here I will show you how to get your team on board with the transformation by getting them to realize and commit to embracing the changes that are needed.

Kick-Start the Journey

After you have the team buy-in to the needed change, it's time to get moving! This part is all about setting lofty goals and grand challenges and formally kicking off the change journey. This is where organizational changes, team adjustment, resource planning, etc. begin. It's where consistent communication begins so teams know what is happening and what progress is being made—and what is expected.

Commit to Staying the Course

In this part of the process, you are learning how things are going and making adjustments as needed. It's about getting the flywheel to move faster and faster. You're learning from the team what's working and what isn't, and you're adjusting constantly.

Nurture Change

I have been through numerous transformation efforts in many organizations, and I have found the heavy lifting of a transformation usually takes anywhere from eighteen to twenty-four months. This is why being persistent is so important. You need to keep up the momentum. Remember, change is the only constant, and you need to consistently find ways to invigorate your change efforts and inspire your teams to continue the journey. That's what the arrows in the above diagram represent—the playbook is continually cycling through the various phases around nurturing change.

People are the key to any organization. Just as you nurture your family, you must nurture your team through this dramatic change. In the busy environments we all find ourselves in, we forget to engage our teams in meaningful ways. Consider this, *"You hire employees, and people show up!"* How are you nurturing your people? Are you treating them merely as employees? Or are you looking at each individual as a person and adjusting your approach in a humanistic, caring way?

Use My Assessment

With all these ingredients and the other elements in mind, take the assessment I've included at my website, mamiefjones.com, or simply scan the QR code below. It will provide you with excellent insight into the type of environment you are in right now or the one you may be considering joining. Remember, not all the ingredients have to be fully in place to make progress. The assessment will provide you with an overall score. Based on your score, you can then determine your next steps.

Buckle up, it's time to move into high gear!

Scan this QR code to access an assessment tool to measure how your environment is ready for change .

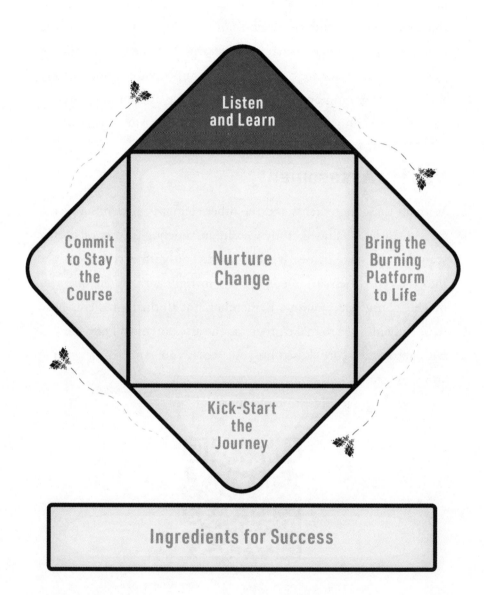

CHAPTER 2

Listen and Learn

I remind myself every morning: Nothing I say this day will teach me anything. So if I'm going to learn, I must do it by listening.

—LARRY KING

Creating the Right Environment

The goal of this stage in the process is to understand what is happening in the workplace on a grassroots level by actively *listening and learning*. As I pointed out in the previous chapter, you are either joining a new company with a new team or taking on a transformation effort with an existing team. With your foundational ingredients in place, as you enter this role, it's important for you to grasp what is *actually* going on. This is not the time to start immediate change. It's the time to be listening, learning, and then only implementing changes once you understand what is needed. You might be tempted to roll up your sleeves and make immediate adjustments, but you need to learn to go *slow* (first) to go *fast*.

Regardless of your situation, you really have one shot to get this Listen and Learn stage of the playbook right. It sets the stage for the rest of the playbook, and you may find yourself coming back to this section as a refresher.

Active Listening

It all begins with *active listening*. I can't stress how important this skill is. You might agree to the idea in theory, and find many others who will likewise agree, but you will be surprised to find how little active listening actually occurs.

Have you ever found yourself in a meeting and there is a moment when someone wants to ask an important question or make a point, and this seems to become their sole focus? As the meeting continues, they are so fixated on this that they miss a significant part of the continuing discussion. This becomes obvious when they get their opportunity to talk. They clearly have not been listening.

> Most people do not listen with intent to understand.
> Most people listen with the intent to reply.
> —STEPHEN COVEY

This results in an ineffective meeting. Many people will only gauge the success of a meeting on whether they got their point across, or whether we came out with a good set of action items, but what makes for a fruitful meeting more than anything else is whether we *listened* and agreed on effective next steps.

Good listeners in a meeting will make notes and draw up questions as the conversation happens. They don't interject at the wrong time, and they wait patiently throughout the meeting until there is a pause where the organizer will ask for other comments or questions. If you aren't the one facilitating the meeting, this is the time to bring up your points. Others in the meeting will often have the same point, and it is best to let others speak first. Use key moments in the meeting to gain more insight on the team or potential issues you might need to address. If your question or point wasn't raised, it shows how well you listened and that your point is well thought out—and this will open up further dialogue.

In meetings where there may be differences of opinion, active listening is even more important. Contention can often stem from a person's emotional attachment to a particular point or idea, and they are "taking up all the oxygen" in the room. This is where diplomatic curiosity comes into play.

I use this term because you learn to disarm people in discussions through a well-thought-out, well-placed question, or an inquisitive comment on a particular topic. The goal is to challenge respectfully by probing for understanding and asking nonthreatening questions. This is not easy to do, but as you practice, you will find it very effective.

As you begin interacting with your team, you will be creating an environment where people will come to know you as an active listener and that you want to *learn* from them in a genuine way. You will hear from your team and the relevant stakeholders, some of which will highlight different aspects of the culture. As you do this, you will begin to understand the organization and the team culture more deeply. All the input you get is incredibly important. You will begin to know your team, and they will begin to know you. Through this process you will also be getting insights into the talent in the organization. You will discover who the influencers are, and all the while, you will be noting important themes that will expand over time and be the foundation of your transformation efforts.

The listening and learning process takes time, but it is worth the effort. You will be pressured to take shortcuts, but you must stay the course. As you get pushback, keep reminding people that you need to *go slow to go fast.* I would tell people this regularly, and it became a motto for the team. The reality is if you do not do your homework properly on your team and the culture, your change effort will be at risk.

Go slow to go fast .

The Current State

Listen and Learn starts with understanding the current state of your organization. As mentioned earlier, the current state is the baseline for measuring improvement. If you do not set a baseline, your goals will not be based on concrete data, and results will be difficult to prove.

Defining the current state is something we often don't spend enough time understanding, nor do we go broad on the areas to improve. Many transformation efforts put very little or no effort at all into this part of the process, thinking change will come just because work is getting started. You can't have a successful transition without honoring the past history of those involved, and you'll struggle with the new state without understanding the current one. This takes time and effort and is easily pushed aside when other priorities keep taking center stage. That's why persistence will be required. People will be asking you to show results quickly, but these results are going to be empty in the long run if you don't do this properly.

There are several aspects to defining the current state. First, the physical environment of the workplace. When I joined Intuit, everybody sat in their own office, behind closed doors. This created a closed culture that was obvious to me as someone new, but not so obvious to everyone else. They would go into their office, shut their door, and wouldn't engage with others, sometimes all day! Communication was very limited. It wasn't relationship-based or healthy, so

I insisted we break down the walls and redo the layout of the office floors entirely. It needed to become a place of collaboration, not a siloed environment. You can imagine how that initially went over like a lead balloon, but once we created collaboration spaces, over time people saw the value and loved it, and we made it fun. That immediately changed one aspect of the culture and began to move us to a new state. So be aware of your physical environment and if there is an opportunity to explore this area.

Next, you want to get to the heart of what drives any culture—and that is the people. Spending time with your team members and understanding what's on their mind is key to the Listen and Learn process. Here are the steps I follow:

1. Talk to every team member.
   - Make it safe—and be genuine.
   - Use a script.
   - Capture quotes.
   - Assemble the themes and quotes.

2. Share what you have learned with your direct leadership team.

3. Prepare for an all-team off-site.

Let's look at each of these in detail.

1. Talk to Every Team Member

I begin by learning about the organization and my new team through thirty-minute meetings with my peers, executives, and every team member. My peer group and the executives give me a sense of what the leadership in the organization thinks about my team. I cast this net out widely. I don't just meet with people in my business unit, but also speak with those in supporting groups or any other group that interfaces with my team across the company. In addition, during these conversations

I'll listen for any other names that come up that carry influence across the organization and have keen knowledge about my team or business unit. I make sure to book meetings with these people as well.

In these discussions, I make sure they feel comfortable voicing their opinions about my team, both good and bad. Here are some examples of the open-ended questions I ask:

1. Tell me what you think of my team. Any impressions you have that you think will be important for me to know and understand?

2. What would be the one or two issues you think are important for me to tackle?

3. What do you need to tell me that I need to be aware of that will help me be successful in my role?

There is no script I follow with this group. These questions are merely designed to facilitate a discussion, give me insight, and build trust. I keep these questions very open-ended and let them do most of the talking while I listen and take notes. You can create your own questions that will suit your context better.

I also spend time with my peers and executives to understand their expectations of me as a new leader. In these discussions, you will hear many different views about your team. You may also hear statements such as, "We've tried this before," or, "I don't think your team is up for any significant change." Be prepared for potential negative comments and take them all in stride.

At the same time, I begin to book thirty-minute employee interviews, managers included. As referenced in the previous chapter, I have a very specific script that I follow in these interviews (below), for all employees, managers included. Front-line employees are my priority because they will tell me what's *really* going on in the organization. I have found in the beginning that managers will frequently tell you what they think you want to hear or gloss over what is not going well, especially if challenges are known in their area(s).

In the process of meeting each team member, I do not let anyone know what I'm going to be discussing or what questions I'm going to be asking. I'm not prescriptive about what I will need from them. I want to see how they think on their feet, and most importantly, I like to watch their body language, which tells me a lot about a person.

If your organization is larger than two hundred employees, it's difficult to meet with all team members. For larger organizations you will need to select a subset of people from each job function, seniority, gender—from the outspoken to the timid, those that are performing well and not so well, etc. You will need HR to help provide an effective cross section of your team. And if you have remote sites, it *requires* an on-site visit. Face-to-face, in-person discussion cannot be replaced.

I conduct these interviews over the course of four to six weeks, depending on the size of the organization. As you book these meetings, you may receive some surprising critique. "Are you *really* meeting with *each* person?" "How are you going to do this with everything else you have to do?" "Is this the best use of your time?" It goes on and on.

But there is nothing more important than interacting with the people that do the work. I've had team members tell me they never had an executive sit down with them to understand their perspectives, let alone learn about them as individuals. Remember these are human beings just like you and me.

HR is key. I do not have them in the actual discussions with team members, but I do brief them consistently through my process. You need to have HR lockstep with you as you listen and learn from the team. You are not asking HR for permission in what you plan to do, but if you bring them along your journey and they understand what you are learning, they will feel part of the process and will most likely become your biggest partner and advocate.

A. Make It Safe–and Be Genuine

People in the workplace have obviously learned to operate under all different kinds of leaders and environments. When a new leader comes in, the team and its individuals have no idea what to expect. Everyone responds differently. They are anxious about what you're going to talk about, and it sends a bit of a ripple through the team. But it's a good ripple effect.

Being genuine is essential in each of your interviews. Remember, you have only one shot at getting this right! People can smell phony a mile away so you must create an environment where they feel safe in providing candid feedback. This only happens when you are actively listening, probing for understanding, and doing very little talking. Change will not come unless you win the trust of your team, and this will happen only when you genuinely listen, probe, understand, and care about their concerns.

The reason why the Listen and Learn process works is because it's a *human-centric approach*. I've been in numerous companies where consultants have been hired to find solutions to complex problems. While the consultants interview a few key people in the organization, it is typically at a very high level, and there is little understanding of the true underlying processes and the company culture. This does not create trust with the teams and does not come across as genuine. You need to come in and create trust with the team where some cynicism may have set in.

> Change will not come unless you win the trust of
> people, and this will happen only when you listen,
> probe, understand, and care about their concerns.

There are situations where you come in and will find the leadership has atrophied and behaviors are entrenched. It will take time for people to start thinking differently and begin taking risks to build an innovative culture. It is incredibly fun and exciting to watch this evolution.

B. Use a Script

When I conduct my thirty-minute interview meetings with my team, I follow a script. You will notice from the script, which I provide below, that there are some personal questions. If people don't feel you are genuine or feel that you have an ulterior motive, they will not open up to you. So I look to honor them in this process by also letting them know my own vulnerabilities. You can't expect others to open up if you're not willing to do so yourself. If you open up about your challenges, you will become more human to them, rather than an executive on high, and be able to connect at a human level. So, I let them know what makes me nervous, anxious, challenged—both at work and at home. As the conversation evolves, you find that there are some similarities in background or home life. This is a great opportunity to connect genuinely and get to know each other.

As you connect with each person, you will begin to see certain themes emerge that describe the current state. This is particularly true when you get to the fourth question below, which focuses on challenges they face. It is human nature for people to talk about their challenges and their opinions on how to address these. These challenges become the themes that will be the focus of your transformation.

It's important to stick to the same script with everyone so they feel they are being treated fairly. Rest assured, they will be talking to one another about the questions you are asking. If you deviate from the script, they have a way of knowing that you are asking different questions compared to someone else, which has happened to me. So

I had to learn to be consistent; otherwise people will feel that you are being unfair or have some other motive. Often by the second week, people come in already knowing what the questions are as they have heard about them from others.

During your interview you need to take copious notes and capture verbatim quotes. I let the team members know that even if they see me writing things down, I am listening. I try to have constant eye contact as much as possible to ensure they know they have my full attention, and I will ask them to slow down if needed.

INTERVIEW SCRIPT

You will see this script is quite simple, but these questions lead to very rich conversations.

1. Tell me about yourself. Where are you from, where did you go to school, what did you study, etc.? (From this question I'm assessing their education, skill level, self-motivation, their excitement for learning, etc.)

2. What projects are you working on? (From this question I get a clear picture of their workload and whether there is adequate resource management.)

3. What are three things that are going well that you don't want to see changed? (From this question I want to understand what they like about the culture, the work, the fun, the recognition—whatever it is they want to keep and not change.)

4. What are three challenges you face? (From this question I typically get the main themes that emerge from the discussions. This is the question where we spend a lot of time talking about what isn't working. You also get most of your verbatim quotes

from this question, and it takes the bulk of the thirty-minute interview. More on this below.)

5. What are your career aspirations? Where do you see yourself in three to five years? (This question gives me insight into their career desires. Do they want to work their way into management? Do they prefer to be an individual contributor, architect, designer? Most people have a hard time with this because they haven't been asked this question and haven't given it a lot of thought. It gets them thinking, and it shows I care about what's important to them.)

6. What would you like to share about yourself and your family? Are you married, have kids, pets? Do you like to travel? (This question provides insight into their home life. Is it busy, complicated, stressful, happy?)

You'll sometimes be shocked by what some people will tell you. They may talk about going through divorce, sick parents, kids with tremendous challenges—it runs the gamut. This also gives me insight to know how to talk to this individual moving forward and show them that I care. I also share these insights with their direct manager if they are not aware of their personal issues, and this will make it easier for them to better support their team members. This is how you start nurturing change. More about this in chapter 6.

Some surprises I have encountered with these questions are eye opening. For example, in the second question above, I ask for a list of all the projects they are working on. In one discussion, I discovered the team member was working on ten projects at the same time. Ten! I think it's obvious that after you work on more than one project there are significant diminishing returns, so ten is insane. This immediately made me realize a major source of frustration: there was little to no resource transparency, and no one knew who was working on what. There was no tool to show what projects were underway and who was dedicated to those projects. Without transparency on what everyone was working on, it created chaos in the environment. It is critical for everything that is required to be done to be laid out so you can start changing the conversations on what is possible. Once people realize that there is a finite number of resources and that it is far more effective to work on one project at a time, the resource debates are reduced. This was the case when I started with Intuit.

I discovered in the same question that everyone was using their own tools to manage projects—Excel, sticky notes, or Microsoft Project, but there was no standard process. This becomes a risk to the business if you can't easily predict what and when you are building and deploying software.

Throughout the interviews you will also begin to get insights into the talent and people's mindsets. You will find incredible talent and a few red flags that you monitor through an upcoming off-site, which is the next step in my transformation playbook. I look for patterns of behavior in questions like what they studied and why they chose the path they've chosen. I'll have some brief follow-up, specific questions, depending on their answer, such as: "Why did you go into technology?" or "Why did you study art but end up in accounting?" The answers to these kinds of follow-up questions will surprise you. I'm not just assessing their education, but I'm assessing how self-motivated they are and how excited they are about learning. I'm also assessing their self-awareness. Can they laugh at themselves? Are they aware of their own strengths and weaknesses? How do they handle their mistakes?

I want people with a growth mindset who are self-motivated and eager to learn new skills. The landscape is always changing in today's workplace. It doesn't matter what industry you are in, innovation and technology are always evolving, and rapidly. You need to have the kind of people who will explore and experiment and take risks with new ideas and drive change. The way people answer these questions will give you tremendous insight into not just their talent, but their personality and room for growth, and how they will respond to the change you will be bringing.

C. Capture Quotes

Quotes define your culture. Take copious notes of what people say and how they express themselves. You want to capture all feedback from stakeholders and team members. You are going to be using this information in the management off-site coming up, which is the next stage in the transformation playbook, which I will outline in the following chapter. In your discussions, people can get emotional, and if you are genuine, they will sometimes use strong language and be very blunt. Your job is to listen and record, not provide any judgment, feedback, or even solutions, other than probing for understanding and validating what you're hearing. It takes a lot for people to open up, and the worst thing you can do is shut them down with your interpretation. This is actually a fun time, and you will learn a tremendous amount through what people tell you.

Here are some examples of quotes from one of my previous engineering team's interviews. These are the kind of quotes you want to capture verbatim:

"I'm stale right now."

"I have implementation fatigue."

"We know what we're doing, but leaders don't."

"*Everything* is a priority."

"Our cycle time is way too long."

"There is no collaboration."

"We don't learn from our mistakes."

"We don't have enough tech skills."

"Every one of our releases causes an outage."

Write your quotes down exactly as you hear them. In my particular case at Intuit, I captured 250 quotes. Some were, of course, much more colorful than the ones above!

Now these quotes are absolutely key to the next step. Once you've collected them and notes from your discussions, it's time to assemble the themes and quotes for your leaders to hear.

D. Assemble the Themes and Quotes

As mentioned above, the fourth question in the script is where most of your themes will emerge. This is because people tend to spend most of their time discussing their challenges. The themes will appear quickly and within the first week become quite apparent.

At Intuit, from the discussions, I assembled eight themes:

1. Infrastructure

2. Communication and collaboration

3. Innovation

4. Development and release process

5. Speed-dedicated teams

6. Talent

7. Application performance

8. Incident management

Your business may have different themes and vocabulary and the number of themes may vary. You will also find themes that will need to be addressed at different points in your transformation, and some themes may need immediate attention that you will work through as a team.

For example, when I arrived at Intuit, we had our internal audit committee auditing our business unit processes. They realized, as I did, that we had no consistent development process, which put the business at risk. We both knew that we would need to tackle this area first because of the risk. While I knew our process would need to be addressed, I also knew this would come up as a theme in our upcoming team off-site. I was well aware of how this would be prioritized by the team, and I had to wait for this next phase of my process to begin remediation. I'll explain this to you shortly.

2. Share What You Have Learned with Your Direct Leadership Team

Once you have formulated the themes, it's time to categorize the quotes into these themes. I place all the quotes on a large visual, which I will share with my leadership team in an all-day meeting. Everything I have learned from the team interviews will also be disclosed in this meeting, which needs to take place where there won't be distractions.

This time can often be difficult as managers may be called out in the quotes, good or bad. For full transparency I insist that all information gets out on the table so the entire leadership team understands the current state and the culture they have created. The read-out of the quotes is really a reflection of their leadership. A good deal of time in the meeting is spent allowing the team to absorb the quotes and the themes. It's very important to create a safe environment for your managers, and they must know that what you share together in this all-day off-site is in the utmost confidence.

In the next chapter, I will unpack this meeting in much more detail. This meeting is essentially the hinge between the Listen and Learn stage and the stage that will follow. You'll see why in the next chapter.

3. Prepare for an All-Team Off-Site

After the all-day leadership meeting above, the next step is to plan a two-day all-team off-site that your leadership team will be involved in putting together. I look for volunteers who want to help with this important event. This off-site effectively consists of two days of exercises and discussions that will reveal the reality of the current state to the entire team. Your leadership team members are not exempt from this process but are very much a part of it. This is a critical part of the transformation process that reveals what I call "bringing the burning platform to life."

Keep your boss informed and tell them you will be having a two-day off-site to bring the full team together and delve into the themes. If you get pushback from your boss on the off-site, this is a good test of their support (one of the ingredients for success). The next chapter will show you how to run this off-site, where you are going to really galvanize the team.

The Biggest Change

As I run through Listen and Learn, I begin to share some of what I'm learning with my peers and my boss. I need to let them understand the skill level of the team and that dramatic changes may be required. They need to know that changes are coming based on all the information I've been gathering. Since you have been documenting what you've learned, you can present some details that may be needed as you move forward.

Remember: *the biggest change you will face in your transformation efforts is the people.* You can't just flip a switch. Transformation is an ongoing process that takes patience and persistence. You will find when you start making talent changes to the team, negative feedback can follow from others. Relationships have been forged over time, and when you disrupt these relationships that serve others well, it results in difficult conversations. Yet as you make positive changes to the team and begin showing results, you will build trust over time with those that challenge you.

> The biggest change you will face in your transformation is the people.

As you implement change, people begin to grow in their existing roles and will discover newfound purpose. In one case we had a specific gentleman who was very negative about their job and environment. He kept pushing back and just had a bad attitude. As we were consistent and transparent in implementing changes, his attitude started to change. It took about eighteen months, and then one day, he walked into my office and shut the door.

"When you first came here," he told me, "I thought to myself, what is this woman doing? I was not a fan. I didn't believe anything you said and did. Everything you insisted we do, I believed was impossible."

I wondered what was coming next.

"But now," he said. "This is the most amazing place to work. I'm so motivated, so inspired, and quite honestly, I have my mojo back."

The Listen and Learn process is a critical step in the playbook. People want to believe there is hope on the horizon, and when you take time to connect with your team in a very real way, their hopes will help propel your efforts. You will get pressure in some cases to move faster, but remember, *go slow to go fast.* This will serve you well as you begin to bring the burning platform to life in the next chapter.

Take Action

Do you have what it takes to drive significant change? Transformation efforts typically take anywhere from eighteen to twenty-four months to get the flywheel momentum established, and it will be difficult and challenging. Not only do you need to drive the transformation process, but you also have to help run the business. These can be very long days, and your calendar will be quite full, even after hours. You have to invest the time to meet the needs of your team and the business.

You will encounter setbacks. I call this, *two steps forward and one step back.* But note you *are* moving forward! As you are persistent in your transformation efforts, you will at times create awkward interpersonal relationships and misunderstandings. People may even call you horrible things behind your back, or to your face, and accuse you of all sorts of agendas. Stick with it. As you make progress, others will start to see what you are doing and will support you. Many of your biggest opponents will become your biggest fans. The positive moments outweigh the negative, and they make it worthwhile.

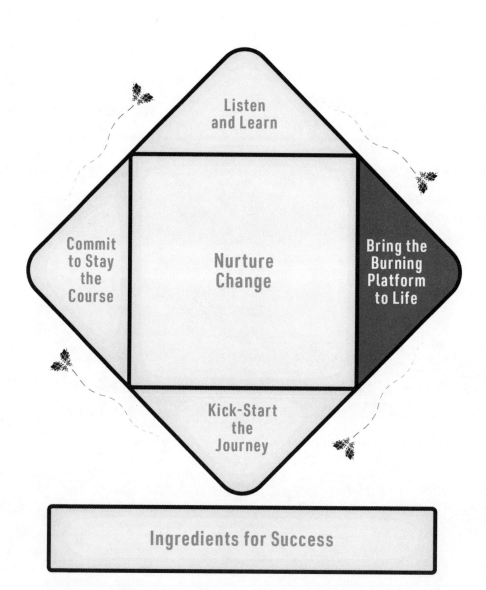

Listen
and Learn

Commit
to Stay
the
Course

Nurture
Change

Bring the
Burning
Platform
to Life

Kick-Start
the
Journey

Ingredients for Success

CHAPTER 3

Bring the Burning Platform to Life

Far and away the best prize that life has to offer
is a chance to work hard at work worth doing.
—TEDDY ROOSEVELT

Capture Hearts and Minds

The Listen and Learn process begins to create the right environment for change. Now it's time to bring the burning platform to life through *capturing hearts and minds.*

The phrase "burning platform" is often used in transformation efforts and refers to getting people to understand for themselves that there is a desperate need for change and no time to waste—that they are standing on a "burning platform." Up to this point, your team knows that you have been brought in to fill a leadership role, but many do not know the extent of what needs to change. Others already know they are on a "burning platform," but they don't know what to do about it.

An Off-Site Will Galvanize the Team

To bring this burning platform to life, the next step is to share all you have learned up to now with the whole team in a two-day off-site. This takes place after your Listen and Learn interviews and after you have documented your themes and quotes.

The objective of the off-site is to get as many team members as possible into the same room for two days and have them understand the current state—and then take ownership of the needed change. It's important to get people out of the office into an environment (that matches your budget) where they are *solely* focused on the transformation agenda. In an office (home or other), it's too easy for people to go to their workspace, take a call, or do other work. This needs to be an "aha" moment for the team. The off-site is a time for people to engage with others and begin building trust and forge new relationships. You will need to make the case for change compelling so that it captures their hearts and their minds to do what will need to be done over the coming months. They must choose to make the change or maintain their own status quo. Whatever the outcome, the off-site makes them realize that they must make a commitment and embrace change—or take another path.

Your job in the off-site is to facilitate what will be an eye-opening experience for your teams. It's going to begin with your leadership team, who you will meet with first before going into the whole team off-site.

Preparing Your Leadership Team

I've learned that you cannot move into the broader team off-site without bringing your leadership team on board. The leadership team needs to understand, at a high level, what is going to be on the agenda—but not all the details or activities. They need to experience the off-site for themselves and will need to make their own commitments to move forward. However, they do need to know that you have a plan, and you have certain requirements for them.

I expect my leaders to be aligned on our next steps. Therefore, we get together for a whole day to review what I learned from the Listen and Learn interviews. You want this session to be conducted in a private room to accommodate the team and their ability to move about. Since some of the information may be sensitive, you want to avoid the possibility of others hearing the content of the meeting. This meeting needs to be conducted without any distractions, so communicating what you're doing with peers and your boss is important.

This all will get them prepared for the larger upcoming team off-site. Here is what you need to do in this meeting to help prepare your leadership team:

A. Set the Tone

People retain 80 percent of what they see—and about 65 percent of people are visual learners.[7] This is why I make everything very visual. I take a large board (approximately 10' x 5') with every quote I gathered from the Listen and Learn sessions and share it with the team. You will adjust the size of your board by the number of quotes and themes.

Then I simply tell them, "This may be difficult for you to see and hear, but this is what your team members are saying about us."

These comments include what their team, peers, and leaders have been telling me. I write the comments verbatim, making sure they can see it all just as it is—without judgment, commentary, interpretation, or trying to make it easier to swallow. I am simply giving them the facts and a way for them to process the information.

---

[7] S. Jawed, H. U. Amin, A. S. Malik, and I. Faye, "Classification of Visual and Non-Visual Learners Using Electroencephalographic Alpha and Gamma Activities," *Frontiers in Behavioral Neuroscience* 13 (2019), https://doi.org/10.3389/fnbeh.2019.00086.

"Now it's just us here in this room," I remind them. "Everything here is highly confidential. We can talk about this openly. This is not to point fingers at anyone; this is to show what our culture is in this organization, a culture you have built and created."

I reveal the board. I tell them, "I'm going to give you thirty minutes to read through these comments and absorb the information."

B. Observe

When I conducted this at Intuit, I had approximately twenty-five leaders in the room. We had over 250 comments on the board to review. How people receive these comments is often extraordinary. Note their facial expressions, their body language. Their emotions will be visible. You will see disappointment and shock. Who is surprised? Who seems to have expected it? Who seems willing to accept it? Who is taking notes? Who may be disengaged?

C. Reflection

I give them thirty minutes to reflect in silence and make their own notes. They need to internalize what it is they are reading. Remember, people internalize differently, so give them time! You may find that more than thirty minutes is needed, so adjust as necessary based on your number of comments. Some will want to react, but you have to ask them to wait until the appropriate time, otherwise it can short-circuit the thought process of others.

D. Dialogue

Once the team has had time to absorb, I ask, "What are your reactions? Do you agree or disagree with these comments about the culture and the environment? Thoughts?"

Be prepared for silence and be patient for the first person to begin the discussion. You just need to be quiet and wait. Don't rush or try to help them begin the conversation. If you just wait, someone will have the courage to speak up eventually, and usually what they say will be quite honest and transparent. Then you will see the discussion begin.

This is a very vulnerable process, but it reveals who on the leadership team has good self-awareness. The dialogue can take anywhere from an hour to an hour and a half. I let people vent as much as they want and make no comments or judgment calls. If they are insecure, they are going to have to deal with that sooner or later. This is an opportunity to help them through that process.

Next I share the themes and ask the team to give their points of view on each of the themes. Part of what is important in this process, when your leaders see these comments and discuss them, they recognize that this didn't come from you. You didn't come up with this. This is what their team members said about them. When they look at the quotes, as we have done, they can pull out the themes that I've pulled out just as easily.

This day in a room brings the burning platform to life for the leadership team. It usually takes another thirty minutes before the discussion simmers down and people begin to ask, "What now?" When the time seems right, I answer that question by giving them a brief overview of what the off-site will be about.

"We're going to talk about the themes that I captured from my interviews," I say. "Your role over the two days will be to participate fully in this in the same way as everyone else. We will discover what we can do together to tackle these issues."

Now they know the themes and will be prepared to support the discussion. Going through each of these themes with this team is important as it gives them a good idea of what's going to come up in the two-day off-site without giving them too much detail. It helps to build trust. They need to know they should not drive the discussions but will provide additive information. Going into the off-site, they realize that they are not supervising their teams or officiating a process, but they are a participant and part of what needs to change in the organization.

It's Time for the Off-Site

At this stage, you have already announced your off-site, booked your venue, and invited the necessary people. Your whole team needs to attend. There may be exceptions depending on remote sites. In order to help make the arrangements as easy as possible, I have included a checklist for you at the end of this chapter. That checklist will ensure you will not forget anything important.

There will be a lot of anticipation around what will be happening at the off-site. There will also be a lot of excitement but also some anxiety. If your team is as spread out as mine has been, you are going to be bringing people in from across the world. You might discover, as I did, that some people have been working together for years and have never met in person! At Intuit, I had teams in four US locations, one in Canada and one in India. I insisted that all North American team members attend in person. Because bringing all India employees to the US was cost prohibitive, I brought a cross section of the team to the off-site, which had never happened and really made them feel valued. This created a lot of buzz around the event and much chatter around the offices!

The off-site happens during the workweek. Do not book this over a weekend as this will not garner any trust from the team. Remember everyone's psyche right now. They know change is coming. You are going to be disrupting their life. They're about to meet people they may have never met in person but may have worked with for years. They don't know what to expect. This is why the venue you choose is incredibly important. It must be a venue that gives the message that they matter and the company cares about them.

Give them a great experience. Have great food, wonderful accommodations, fantastic entertainment. You can't go on the cheap here. The minute they walk in, they must feel taken care of. I arrange buffet breakfast stations, coffee, followed by snacks, then a buffet lunch, more snacks in the afternoon, and an incredible dinner. For Intuit, we arranged a special evening experience in a private room in a fabulous restaurant, with great entertainment. Since we were in a hotel, they had freedom to use the facilities as they liked. Everything that you do must convey the message: "We're investing in you. We will treat you well. We're not fooling around." You want them to come back from this off-site saying, "Wow!" They should get back to their offices incredibly energized and motivated and feeling as if they are part of a team that is going to do great things together.

The room where most of the activity will take place in the day needs to be sufficiently large for a lot of activity and moving around, with large tables, as well as space for plenty of snacks and refreshments. At Intuit, we booked a venue that allowed us to set up in what was essentially a large ballroom. The room setup included eight tables that reflected the themes that I captured. You can adjust the number of your themes based on your interviews and comments; they may not always total eight—but whatever the number, the tables match. When everyone arrives at the event, they have pre-assigned seating and are formed in Agile (scrum) groups. Of course, we don't call them that and don't tell anyone that this is what we're doing. They are not aware of this, and we keep this to ourselves until the end of the event.

What Agile means in practice will differ according to your business, but in our business at Intuit, it essentially meant that each table had at least one leader, architect, designer, engineer, project manager, and tester. You should also have a mix of seniority at each of your tables. It must include a mix of men and women. You need to be very selective of who sits at each table and make sure each function in your team is represented. For us, each table had ten people. Many of these people had never worked together before, or if they had, never in this kind of arrangement.

You kick off the event with an exercise that takes the team members out of their comfort zone. One such exercise includes a bucket under their tables full of wacky props such as kooky hats, feather boas, crazy glasses, and whatever other silly things you can think up. I let them discover these buckets for themselves and love seeing the "Are you kidding me?" looks on people's faces as they discuss what on earth these props could mean. I'll watch and take mental notes of reactions. There will be some excited responses, some groans, some apprehension, and a lot of expectancy. The buckets are all centered around what they are going to do next. Once everyone has settled, I tell them what it's all about.

"You're going to create an advertisement for the company," I say. "There are some rules around this activity," I then explain.

First, the ad must deliver a marketing message specific to the mission and goals of the company.

Second, it must deliver a customer benefit.

Third, it has to be delivered in thirty seconds to one minute, no more.

Fourth, every prop in the bucket *must* be used.

Fifth, every member at the table *must* participate.

The winning team receives an award. Back in 2012, for Intuit, this was a day off (and they could pick the day). A remote team might be motivated differently. Whatever award you choose should be meaningful and make the effort worthwhile.

The buckets should also include props relevant to your company. For Intuit, we included pencils, pens, big charts, accounting graphs, and the like. Team members are then given thirty minutes to come up with their ad.

I recruited my boss and executive peers to be the judges. This is important. Often the leaders of an organization don't interact meaningfully with front-line employees. This exercise breaks down some of those walls. When your team sees that you've arranged high-profile people to be part of this, it speaks volumes about you and the organization's leadership and their commitment to the transformation. I got the general manager and all the vice presidents to sit in chairs and judge the advertisements. We also arranged video recordings. This brought things to a whole new level—many couldn't believe that their company leaders were going to judge their advertisement! What's also great about this is the leaders have a tremendous amount of fun, and it really helps to break down barriers and let everyone get to know each other better.

Why start this way? Why set things up with the tables and the teams and the crazy props and the judges?

1. It gets people out of their comfort zones. They have to do something crazy and fun, and they don't have a lot of time to overthink it! You can observe and see how they participate, how they think on their feet, which gives you considerable insight into their creativity and mindset.

2. It gets people to think differently. They have to get creative and think out of the box because there is a time limit.

3. It's good for them to learn how to work in a scrum environment, even if they don't know what that is yet. They will discover this later.

Now everyone has their minute-to-win-it, and it really breaks the ice! We then take a break, and all the leaders get to engage with the people, which also helps them to get out of their comfort zone. Everyone has fun, and the leaders get to present the awards.

This is not just about breaking the ice, but it also helps you gauge who the team players and emerging potential leaders are. Notice who is complaining. Who is refusing to have any fun at all? Who are the introverts? Who surprises you? Who are the ones that take charge and are natural leaders? What do they all do under pressure? Who seems to not want to have anything to do with anybody in this room? As you track these behaviors, it gives you a new level of understanding of your talent.

Time to Get Down to Business

Once we've enjoyed ourselves, had fun, and the leaders have engaged personally with the teams, it's time to let them go and move to the next step of the off-site.

Remember, every table has a theme relevant to those you categorized during the Listen and Learn process. Every team at every table will now own the theme of their table. Your themes may be different than the eight I found at Intuit, depending on your business, but you'll note that several of these may fall broadly under People, Process, and Platform (technology). But remember: don't tell anyone these details. Allow them to have their own "aha" moments.

A quick reminder—the themes we had for Intuit were:

1. Infrastructure

2. Communication and collaboration

3. Innovation

4. Development and release process

5. Speed-dedicated teams

6. Talent

7. Application performance

8. Incident management

I go through each of these themes and explain why they were chosen and what I have learned in the past few months. I highlight that this is what everyone in this room told me are the biggest problems. I simply ask: "Did I get it right?" This is where you will get a lot of head nodding.

Then I encourage them. "Now, we're going to tackle each of these themes as a team. Together, we're going to work out what we need to do next to address every one of these themes."

Each table has a flip chart. Each team has thirty minutes to discuss and write on the chart three things:

1. Define the problem (related to the theme).

2. Define what we need to do to solve the problem.

3. Define priorities to improve.

This is another opportune moment to observe. Who emerges as the leader or spokesperson of the group? Who picks up the pen to record thoughts? Who organizes the team? You'll again see the natural leaders emerging.

It's important to remember that you have to be very observant during this entire process. It's not just about the outcome but also about understanding the people you are working with. Make sure they have name tags! You need to learn everyone's name and speak to them directly. Good leaders know that people like to be called by their name—it makes them feel heard, seen, and validated. It also helps you to make your points more strongly when you use their name. Whenever I speak to people, I will say their name. Immediately it gives them a sense of pride, and they know that I remember them and am listening to them.

> Good leaders know that people like to be called by their name—it makes them feel heard, seen, and validated.

Once the thirty minutes are up, we have everyone switch tables. That way, every team has an opportunity to provide input on all the themes. This exercise takes up the bulk of the remaining first day.

You will begin to see them having very rich conversations with each other. They will take what another table said and expand on it, putting in more detail. By the end of the exercise, you will have a massive amount of information.

Then it's time for the evening break. I tell them before we break that there will be homework for the evening, and I give them their team instructions, which are to compile the information in a Power-Point that:

1. Defines the problem of the theme

2. Summarizes the priorities to improve

3. Proposes next steps

I remind them that everyone must participate in the homework assignment. They need to pick their scribe and their presenter and be ready to present first thing in the morning.

Then I tell them that, before the homework, we're going to have a fabulous dinner, but the entertainment is a surprise. I always arrange unusual, unique musical entertainment. Music is something everyone enjoys. Liven it up. Book a private room in a restaurant outside the hotel if needed as it should feel as if it's away from the intensity of the off-site.

After this is done, they are free to work on their presentations wherever they would like in the hotel, with refreshments, coffee, etc. available to them.

In the Morning

Eight people now must get up and deliver to the entire team what they summarized from all the feedback. It's interesting to note who they choose to make the presentation. It starts to become obvious who everyone naturally respects. Also note their presentation and communication skills.

As everyone does their round, you find they will receive a lot of applause and people saying, "Great job!" The team spirit is usually quite good at this point.

Once all the presentations are complete, you bring their attention to a large board that lists each of the themes.

"We need to now decide which of these we tackle first," I say to them. "Can we do all eight?"

"No," is the response. Eight is too much.

"Can we do six?"

"No."

"How about four?"

"Maybe."

"OK. Can we think about three?"

You will usually find that the majority seem comfortable taking on three. People intuitively know that three major projects or tasks are about as much as they can handle.

Then each person is given three sticky dots.

"Take your dots and put them against the themes you think we should tackle," I tell them. "You can only choose three, no more."

What's important here is they get to choose which of all the issues they feel needs the most attention first. You will see quickly which theme gets the most stickers. I know from experience that the three themes they will prioritize will be People, Process, and Platform, but not necessarily in this order. But I've told no one this. If I did, they wouldn't believe it anyway, but more importantly it would sabotage the process. The magic of this is everyone gets to discover and see it all for themselves.

In my particular case at Intuit, most of the notes ended up prioritizing People/Talent first. What I found interesting about this was they were essentially saying about themselves that they lacked the talent to correct the issues! They were making the claim that they, themselves, were the problem, and a course correction was needed!

Process came in second, and Platform/Infrastructure was third.

Now, when all the sticky notes are on the board, I have everyone stand back. We draw a circle around the biggest collection of sticky notes. This helps people visualize again where the majority of people believed the most attention was needed. Again, everyone stands back and we simply look at it. It's easy to see now what is most important.

"Let's break it down to the top three."

And you can guess it, even if you've put a different name on it, that these will be around People, Process, and Platform.

To conclude the event, I ask the team some simple questions.

"Do we all believe we have big problems to solve?"

Wait for the response. "Yes!"

"Should we give it a shot?"

Wait for the response. "Yes!"

I then ask, "Do you think we can solve all three?"

Wait for the response. It's always an emphatic, "Yes!"

Note that I'm not telling anyone what to do. This is important. It's a process of self-discovery and self-awareness. You are merely facilitating their own commitment to going forward. That's how you bring the burning platform to life—you let people internalize it. They hear their peers saying the same thing, making the same commitments. It's a powerful thing to witness as they all come together. Everyone agrees that the process is broken. Everyone agrees that how they've been doing things is not working. Everyone agrees we don't have the right talent. Everyone agrees we need a better platform. Throughout the off-site, everyone has had their chance to put their thoughts and emotions and frustrations down on paper and be part of the team in deciding what needs to be done next. You have captured their hearts and their minds!

It's now your turn to summarize the off-site by reminding them of the discussions, outcomes, and commitments made.

"We're going to do this," I will say, and highlight the next steps they suggested we take.

"Yes, we've got to do this," you will hear them agree. As mentioned earlier, at Intuit, we had an internal audit underway, and we all agreed we had to tackle our Process challenges first. But instead of me telling the team we have to prioritize our processes, they made that decision together.

Now is also the time to introduce an Agile methodology as a way of working together going forward. For most people this has been an inspiring process, so it's good to let them know this was a deliberate effort to form them into Agile teams for them to get a taste of what it was like to work as a team in this way. This wasn't random—this was all quite deliberate!

"Look at your table and look at our process. You're an Agile team! And look at what you were able to do together, having never worked like this before!" I will say.

At Intuit, when they picked Process, we all agreed to adopt scrum. Having seen it in action, it was so much easier for them to grasp what that meant. While they voted to tackle our process, there will still be some cautiousness.

"Please don't make us do this on our own," they said. "Please bring in people to teach us how to learn in this new process and give us the right tools to be successful." I agreed and made the commitment to bring in experts and provide the right tools for them to be successful.

I'll finish off the off-site by saying something like this: "You all did an incredible job! And now we are kick-starting this journey and are going to start picking up the pace. We'll begin by establishing new aspirational goals."

We don't set these goals at the off-site but immediately afterward. Goals will be set for the overall team, for each of the teams, and then down to each individual. I will coordinate this with my leadership team next. But it's good to let them know now that there will be new goals established in the coming days.

Change forces us to grow. I have found that regardless of how much people resist change, they are usually grateful once the change is underway, and they see progress being made. Again, this process is actually all about helping people see their environment with new eyes. Many people will *need* to leave to grow in their own careers. Some people don't even realize when they are stuck!

Your role now will move into being a coach, setting high and lofty goals and refusing to accept any behavior that points to an inability to imagine a different future, giving everyone what they need to achieve the objectives the whole team has agreed to tackle. It is through this off-site meeting that you have aligned your team.

Meeting Back with Your Leadership Team

As I mentioned at the beginning of the chapter, your leadership team needs to be part of this process from the beginning to the end. Like the rest of the team, they need to come to the necessary conclusions for themselves. It's good to meet with them the next day while things are still fresh in everyone's mind and begin to set the needed goals.

It's the overall team goals that must be set first, before you set the specific team and individual goals. I expect my leadership team to drive the new expectations and goals, then cascade them down.

In the next chapter we will outline how to set these goals, how to track them, and how to communicate them. It is these goals that will kick-start your journey into high gear. The Listen and Learn process and the subsequent off-site, where we bring the burning platform to life, is where we go slow. But now it's time to go fast! And we move into high gear!

CHECKLIST FOR THE OFF-SITE:

1. Select and book a venue for accommodations and meeting room—for local team members, pick a venue that is centrally located so travel time is considered.

2. Design meeting room with hotel liaison (ballroom).

   ☐ *Round tables with chairs with floor-length tablecloths to accommodate ten people.*

   ☐ *Determine decorations for room, tables, etc. Hotel liaison will help with this.*

   ☐ *Create decorations for themes (on the wall, hanging from the ceiling, tents on the table are all options).*

☐ *Order audiovisuals for room: projector, screen, podium, podium microphone and handheld microphones for open discussions, video recording for commercials, etc.*

☐ *Select and play upbeat music in the meeting room when the team enters and at all breaks.*

☐ *Tables needed for food and snacks.*

☐ *Table and chairs for executive coordinators.*

3. **Create team table assignments.**

4. **Select and order food with hotel liaison (really important) and ensure all food options include options for vegetarians, vegan, paleo, keto, gluten-free, etc.**

☐ *Breakfast with coffee and continental breakfast.*

☐ *Morning snacks (be creative).*

☐ *Lunch buffet.*

☐ *Afternoon snacks (be creative).*

☐ *Dinner in the venue or adjacent to the venue.*

☐ *Have goodies on the tables like candies, stress balls, etc.*

5. **Materials needed for meeting.**

☐ *Name tags.*

☐ *Flip charts for each table.*

☐ *Writing utensils for each table.*

☐ *The name of the theme on the table should be very visible—tents.*

☐ *Pens and writing tablets for each team member on the table.*

☐ *Create a large board to highlight themes and for the team to select the top three themes.*

☐ *Sticky circles for the team to select top three themes.*

☐ *Create PowerPoints for the team to work from (their homework the first night).*

☐ *Create PowerPoints to give team instruction for activities (commercial). This is included in the overall PowerPoint for the entire off-site.*

☐ *Create overall PowerPoint to show agendas, and it runs for the entire off-site with timing to stay on track. Ensure ample breaks.*

☐ *Buy props and bins for the commercials and have these under the theme tables (whacky items along with appropriate props to create commercial based on industry).*

6. Arrange for executives to attend the meeting for the commercial and judging portion.

☐ *Have awards created for first, second, and third places.*

7. Arrange for entertainment (after dinner on the first night).

8. Have at least two coordinators in the meeting at all times. Distribute name tags, create all the PowerPoints, work with the hotel liaison for food timing and snacks, address issues as they arise, etc. This is typically executive assistants who address all issues and help keep the meeting on track.

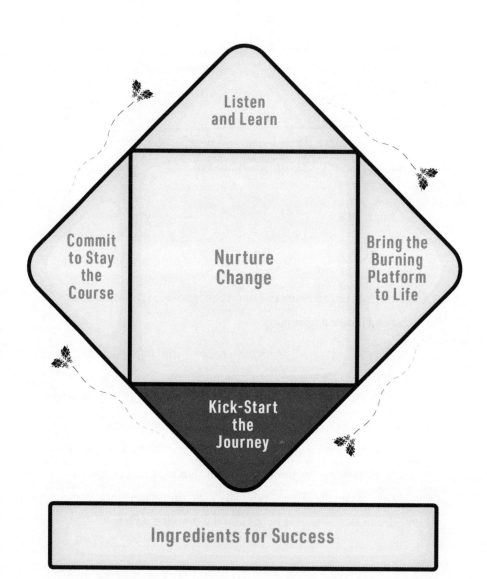

CHAPTER 4

Kick-Start
the Journey

Coming together is a beginning;
keeping together is progress;
working together is success.

—HENRY FORD

People, Process, Platform

Up until now, you have engaged in active listening, done your homework, understood where many of the challenges were, have gained a good understanding of the culture, and taken all that you learned to your off-site. Here you brought the burning platform to life and captured the commitment from your team on what needs to be tackled. If all has gone well, they are on board, and it's time to springboard off that momentum.

Kick-starting the journey is all about goal setting. In the off-site, through a process of self-discovery, everyone has agreed to address your top three pressing issues, which in my experience always end up being People, Process, and Platform. The task before you now is to get as many people galvanized and inspired around what needs to be done, which begins with setting clear, aspirational goals.

In the previous chapter I presented eight themes that I took to the team at Intuit, which were the result of listening and learning. These were:

1. Infrastructure (platform)
2. Communication and collaboration
3. Innovation
4. Development and release process (process)
5. Speed-dedicated teams
6. Talent (people)
7. Application performance
8. Incident management

While there can be a bit of overlap between the themes, by the end of our off-site we specified our Talent, Development, and Release Process, and Infrastructure as needing the most attention. In short, we needed to address our People, Process, and Platform. These three pillars uphold transformation in any business. By focusing on your People, your Process, and your Platform, which you will need to do simultaneously, you will find your other challenges also begin to show progress.

It's now time to kick-start the journey by making bold moves and taking big swings. This revolves around setting aspirational goals within each of the three pillars of People, Process, and Platform. I find the hardest part of implementing change is the need to upgrade talent, which is the focus of the People pillar. It requires hiring the right leadership and talent, and it requires setting skill and behavioral goals. As you introduce these changes, some people will struggle and need to adapt to a new way of thinking, working, and learning. For many, these changes can introduce uncertainty, which can trigger a stress response; for others it is a welcome change and infuses excitement. There are still others that will experience anxiety when they realize they will need to improve their skills, adopt new processes, and lose their comfortable routines.

As you learned in the previous chapter, the team voted on "People" as the leading issue that needed to be addressed. Interestingly, the People pillar, which is about upgrading your talent, is also my first primary focus in any transformation I undertake—keeping in mind that Process and Platform will begin in parallel.

Upgrading Talent

There are three areas of focus that need to be addressed as you begin your talent upgrade:

1. Your leadership team

2. Setting aspirational goals

3. Addressing behaviors

1. Your Leadership Team

The book *Good to Great*, by Jim Collins, highlights why some companies succeed over others in the same industries. Collins notes that over a sustained number of years, it first comes down to leadership and the people they serve. "The executives who ignited the transformations from good to great did not first figure out where to drive the bus … they *first* got the right people on the bus (and the wrong people off the bus) and then figured out where to drive it."[8]

---

8   Jim Collins, "First Who – Get the Right People on the Bus," First Who, accessed December 18, 2023, https://www.jimcollins.com/article_topics/articles/first-who.html.

It's about the people and how to lead differently with exceptional leadership talent that can lead with drive and compassion.

I begin by assessing my direct leadership team, which typically ranges anywhere from six to ten leaders, depending on the size of the organization. Yours will vary based on your organizational structure. I put my primary focus on the leadership team as they will be the drivers of the bus that take us to our new destinations. In the information technology (IT) industry, it is crucial to have brilliant IT leaders who have had experience driving fundamental change in the three pillars of People, Process, and Platform. Because you have been brought in to lead extraordinary change, the incumbent leadership team may or may not possess the needed skills to drive this kind of change. This is where you will have to begin to make tough people decisions.

2. Setting Aspirational Goals

At the off-site there was enthusiasm and a lot of head nodding, but when the rubber meets the road, things can get bumpy. Setting aspirational goals helps people understand your high expectations. As previously discussed, for some of your team members, this will give a renewed and exciting sense of purpose, while for others it will create anxiety. For the latter, the cause can be any number of things: a sense of the unknown, questions around whether they are safe in their job, doubts about whether they can make the change journey, or if they have the skills necessary to be successful. You will need to nurture the team through the change process, inspiring and encouraging them along the way. We will discuss this more in chapter 6.

Your objective is to get as many team members as possible to join you in the change journey. You start this by setting very strategic, aspirational goals—what Jim Collins and Jerry Porras call BHAGs

(Big Hairy Audacious Goals).[9] These are outrageous ventures that inspire people to think and dream bigger than they have ever before. If the goals are lofty enough, even reaching 70 to 80 percent of the goal will be a big win.

> Your objective is to get as many team members as possible to join you in the change journey.

As you plan your talent update, you of course want the best talent in the world. I look for talent that is highly skilled in their area of discipline. They need to be self-motivated, risk takers, courageous, and curious and have a learning mindset. We set two types of goals that help to assess the existing talent against these attributes: (a) skill and (b) behavior. For each of your BHAGs, you set these with your leadership team, who is responsible for cascading these to the teams and then down to each individual. These goals should also ladder up to the business unit goals and the broader company goals. I find when you focus on delivering your BHAGs, the business goals typically take care of themselves.

a) Skill Goals

Whatever industry you are part of, you need to look at a broad array of skill set goals. Here is a list of some of the expert skill sets we looked for, bearing in mind that this was the IT industry.

1. Technical

2. Release management

3. Architecture

---

9   J. Collins and J. I. Porras, *Built to Last: Successful Habits of Visionary Companies* (New York, NY: Harper Collins, 2004).

4. Automated testing

5. Agile/Scrum

6. Resource management

7. Program management

8. Business acumen

9. Security and fraud

10. Operations

This is not an exhaustive list. If you were in marketing, for example, your goals may include search engine optimization (SEO) skills, copywriting, web development, etc. Whatever your industry, build your aspirational goals around the skills needed for the future.

Once the aspirational goals are established, my direct leaders and second-level leaders formulate individual goals for each member of their team that must ladder up to the aspirational goals. To ensure everyone understands what is expected, I communicate these goals broadly and frequently through several communication mechanisms. This includes skip level meetings, off-sites, a weekly note, pizza lunches, etc., which I will explain in more detail in the next two chapters. Once the individual goals are established, we begin to monitor and report our progress through the same communication mechanisms, and to our teams and leaders. By providing frequent and consistent communication, a healthy organization and a culture of open transparency begins to be built.

At Intuit, one example of setting skill goals was in our application testing discipline. Our testers only knew how to do manual testing. They created a checklist of every permutation they could think of to test all features of the application for defects or "bugs." Any time changes were made to the application (which was frequently) they had to start the manual test process all over again. It's very inefficient to test applications this way, and it consumes an enormous amount of time and resources. So we set an aspirational goal for the team: move from 100 percent manual testing to 90 percent automated testing. What this meant for the team was testers would be required to learn and write automated test scripts, which called for coding skills. This was a difficult decision, but it was necessary to deliver better applications to our customers and to better utilize our limited resources.

Of course, it's not a matter of telling people the goal and leaving them to figure it out on their own! We offered extensive training courses for everyone on the team to learn new automated testing skills. Not everyone was able to meet this goal, and many either left the organization or moved to a different organization that could better utilize their skills. Over an eighteen-month period, we moved from 100 percent manual testing to 90 percent automated testing. This was a dramatic change to the organization, but one that was essential to providing bug-free products to our customers, reduce our inefficiencies, and build a more resilient team. Furthermore, as the test organization became engineering focused, they were able to move between two disciplines of testing and engineering, offering additional career opportunities.

b) Behavioral Goals

With the right mindset, new skills can typically be learned with the proper training, but behavioral goals are far more difficult to address as they can often appear subjective. This is where coaching becomes important to gauge a person's willingness to engage. Here are some examples of the behavioral goals I set:

1. Demonstrates positive team participation.

2. Has a high "say/do" ratio (Do they do what they say they will do?).

3. Has a commitment to deliverables, no matter what it takes.

4. Exhibits constructive meeting behaviors (listening/contributing).

5. Exhibits a learning and self-motivated mindset.

6. Possesses a positive attitude and demonstrates positive body language.

7. Is prepared for meetings, stand-ups, one-on-ones.

8. Experiments and takes risks.

9. Challenges respectfully.

Etc.

The behavior goals being developed are communicated as clear expectations to the team. The more transparent you are about the behavior goals, the better people will understand and know what is expected. As a result, several people may leave the organization of their own accord as they realize they cannot, or they aren't willing, to make the leap.

When I speak of behaviors, I am referring to mindsets and attitudes and work habits. How is the team member behaving in meetings? Do they grumble under their breath? Are they naysaying? Do they push back on every endeavor? Are they avid learners? Do they exhibit a growth mindset? Do they engage in healthy conflict and communication, or are they passive-aggressive? Are they rude and disengaged? How are they delivering against their goals? These are the kinds of questions you need to be discussing with your leadership team and they, in turn, with their leaders and managers.

Your leadership team is not exempt from demonstrating the right behaviors. Some may not be up for the task. If I find a leader is not demonstrating or addressing behavioral issues, this becomes a coaching opportunity for correction or other action.

3. Addressing Behaviors

In my experience, there are five broad categories of adverse behaviors that impede a team's ability to succeed in transformational efforts. These will be hard to deal with, and you need to spot them quickly and address them swiftly. Do not allow them to linger.

1. When people say one thing but do another.

2. When people privately grumble about the work environment but do not have the courage to challenge in appropriate ways.

3. When people try to use the rules of the company to create obstructions. For example, they might report you to HR, citing ethical concerns. It's important to keep your head cool and your assessment of the circumstance objective in these situations.

4. When people hide what is really going on and tell you a false status.

5. When people group together and create a clique that, together, refuses to do things that are being asked of them.

Again, remember you are there to help grow and develop individuals. Many of these behaviors are exhibited by people who might not fully know the source of their own frustration and how they are stunting their own growth. Think about how what you're doing is disrupting their lives. That will help you stay objective as you consider the fears that people might have, such as:

1. They are discovering for themselves that they might be in the wrong job.

2. They are fearful they will be exposed as unskilled.

3. They feel you are getting in the way of their ambitions or routines. They mapped out a clear career path that you are now disrupting.

4. They may not have had any ambitions at all and are now fearful that a comfortable situation is being upended.

These are all normal, human reactions to change. The trouble is these behaviors and hidden fears can pull everyone else down, plus they are not helpful to the team or the individual. This is why you need to make people aware of their own behavior and what they need to do to course correct. It's important to bring these things to light and have critical coaching conversations. As you and your leaders work with each team member, you can inspire them to rise to the occasion or agree to help them explore other opportunities.

The latter isn't the objective because so much time, expense, and care goes into building strong teams, but there are times when it's the best outcome for both parties. I've had many people in this situation who, after a long and arduous exit process, call me and tell me how much happier they are, having made the collective decision to move elsewhere. One case involved a highly skilled individual we had to let go. Many people didn't want to see him go because it's hard to lose someone who is highly skilled. Every business invests a great deal in their employees, and when good talent leaves, an organization may find it difficult to adjust. It took months before we mutually agreed that he needed to find a different role or move to another company. After he left, sometime later, I received a phone call from him.

"I just want to thank you," he said. "I'm in my new job and loving it. I realize now just how much I was in the wrong place. I had been doing the same thing over and over again. Quite frankly, I was in a rut and didn't want to change. But now I'm in a role much more aligned with my skill set, and I'm re-energized! Thanks for giving me the push I needed."

When behavioral issues arise, your role and that of your leaders is to coach or help guide people to find something more suitable outside the organization.

Remember, there will be some other wonderful surprises as well. Many people you think are not capable will rise to the occasion and often shock you with their incredible skill and potential. I give every person on the team the opportunity to succeed. Many absolutely flourish when given the opportunity to do so.

Finding Alignment

Jack Welch once said, "You build the best team, you win."[10] I'm grateful for many of Welch's insights that have been developed into what is often called the "Performance-Values Matrix."[11] A 2012 study from Bradley University analyzed the core components of Welch's Performance-Values Matrix and concluded that it is a highly accurate way to enhance performance in an organization, compared to other approaches.[12] I've taken some of the common approaches to this method by various management firms, along with Welch's concepts, and made a few tweaks of my own.

---

10   Nadia Goodman, "Jack Welch on How to Manage Employees," *Entrepreneur*, October 5, 2012, https://www.entrepreneur.com/growing-a-business/jack-welch-on-how-to-manage-employees/224604.

11   Tendekai Dzinamarira, "The Performance Values Match Matrix (Jack Welch)," accessed December 18, 2023, https://www.12manage.com/forum.asp?TB=performance_appraisal&S=71.

12   Aaron Buchko et al., "Values-Based Management or the Performance-Values Matrix: Was Jack Welch Right?," *Journal of Business and Leadership* (January 1, 2012), https://doi.org/10.58809/kupd4878.

The Performance-Values Matrix

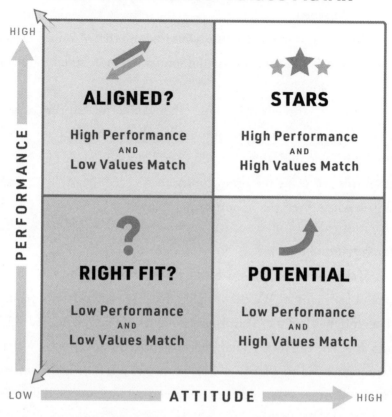

HIGH

PERFORMANCE

ALIGNED?

High Performance
AND
Low Values Match

STARS

High Performance
AND
High Values Match

RIGHT FIT?

Low Performance
AND
Low Values Match

POTENTIAL

Low Performance
AND
High Values Match

LOW ⬛⬛⬛ **ATTITUDE** ⬛⬛⬛➡ HIGH

Many different management firms appear to alter this model.[13]

Many use the model to assess how closely the behaviors of an individual match to a belief in the organization's core values. In my case, I use it in talent discussions to see how well the individual's skills match their behavior in the team. With my direct leadership team, we will rate our staff accordingly by simply putting individuals into these quadrants.

Everyone wants those who fall in the right-hand quadrants on their team (Stars and Potential). They match the desired skills and

---

13   Tendekai Dzinamarira, "The Performance-Values Match Matrix (Jack Welch),"
12manage.com, accessed December 18, 2023, https://www.12manage.com/forum.
asp?TB=performance_appraisal&S=71.

behaviors. Of these two, you obviously want the people who exhibit the best talent, mindset, and attitude—your Stars. Second to that, you are looking for those with potential (or desired attitude)—their skills might be low at this point, but they are willing to learn and improve and are on board with what is needed.

These two pools of talent embody the core talent of the organization. They will be your change agents. Recognize early that many people in the organization desperately want change. It's not always obvious who these people are, but you need to be looking for them. It's rewarding when you see someone emerge from the team who is delivering unanticipated results. These wonderful surprises will keep you motivated—be patient, they will come.

Now you need to evaluate the others located in the left-hand quadrants. This is where it will get more difficult. Do you have a top skilled individual who, regrettably, exhibits behaviors that don't meet your goal expectations? They are not aligned. Challenging their behavior in the organization can often result in significant pushback from others as they are afraid to lose the important skills these individuals possess. Furthermore, people in this quadrant are very comfortable with their own conduct and don't see why they need to change or improve. They may also possess a great deal of influence and respect from others because of their skill. However, you must make your own assessment of the people that fall into this quadrant and make the necessary decisions. Often, they need to exit the organization.

The last group located in the bottom-left quadrant have a low skill level and exhibit poor behavior and mindsets. Sometimes they might exude confidence, but they clearly don't carry competence. They are simply not the right fit and need to leave the organization.

Remember, you're not making a moral judgment of a person; you are simply looking for consistent alignment to the culture you are working to build.

Skill and behavioral goals are based on where people fit in the quadrants. The behavioral goals that you establish are then turned into developmental goals for each individual. The developmental goals must be actionable and measurable (just as the skill goals). Managers help each team member establish development goals that are monitored and discussed in one-on-ones. Where there are challenges in these goal areas, more frequent meetings to course correct will be needed. I will provide more detail on how to conduct such meetings and how to keep your finger on your progress.

Transforming Your Process

At Intuit, one of our biggest and most pressing needs was to improve our software development process. We needed to move from a chaotic way of developing software to one that was predictable and repeatable. For us, this meant we had to move from a "Waterfall-like" process to Agile, specifically scrum. This required a significant shift and new skill sets. It was a major pressure point because Intuit's internal audit committee identified our business unit as being a risk to the company because of our inconsistent and unpredictable software delivery.

I also knew that changing our process would be a catalyst for positive change and took this pressure point as an opportunity to accelerate this change. While Agile is especially popular in the tech and software world, where its principles and methodologies were originally formed and pioneered in the early 2000s, it has become an exceptionally powerful approach adopted in many other industries as well. I believe any Agile methodology to be a core transformational opportunity for organizations looking to adapt to the increasingly fast-paced, always-changing business landscape. The advantages are many: a customer-centric approach that encourages team collaboration and adaptability, and it develops healthy cross-functional teams. By its nature it pushes for continuous improvement and empowers employees to make quick and better decisions. It's also data-driven and highly dynamic. As you will see, our transformation was centered around this new process.

In addition to changing our process, I had to put a spotlight on the lack of rigorous resource management. As I learned in the one-on-one interviews with the team during the Listen and Learn phase, there was no deliberate process for managing the team's resources. It was a conglomeration of different approaches, which led to difficulties in communicating and executing thorough and accurate project management. We needed to bring urgent transparency and visibility to this issue.

We started by documenting a visual representation of what each team member was working on, which we shared with senior leadership. It was eye-opening for the team because it showed where resources were being applied and how chaotic our development process was, which was one of the reasons we were not delivering consistently. With the leadership team understanding the chaotic nature of our resource allocations, using this data we did several things. We had our product management team align on one prioritized list of all projects. We then applied all development resources against the project list, assigning team members to one project until all resources were accounted for. Because there were not enough resources to cover all the projects that were underway, this resulted in the product management team having to stop or delay projects and halting what we call "shadow projects." These are projects where individuals come to development team members and ask them to do a small project on the side as a favor—a project that is not on anyone's radar nor on a prioritized list. When we delayed and stopped these projects, enthusiasm across the teams was created because they saw that we were helping to improve their work environment.

All the teams were now formed into scrum teams, and we started to roll out our new process. Because I had the support of the audit committee and senior leadership, I was able to move forward with the scrum rollout without a great deal of resistance from my peers and other team members. This was a radical departure from how we were used to developing software, and we had to smooth over some ruffled feathers in the beginning stages.

When making this kind of process change, there is typically an S-curve experience, which basically means you need to "go slow to go fast." The S-curve shows a new process from its slow early beginnings to an acceleration phase. As the process matures, it moves to stabilization over time, as was the case for us. I needed to reassure our teams that this was normal. I also told them there would be an initial dip in productivity, but they needed to trust that once the teams were up to speed, our speed of development would actually accelerate.

All of this is why the initial BHAG we set was to have *every* team in our organization migrate to scrum within a year. You might recall that during the off-site in the previous chapter, we gave everyone a taste of how scrum worked. They were on board moving to this new process but asked us not to have them figure it out on their own. The first step to achieving this was to bring in outside experts to provide training, coaching, and certification for all teams. At the same time, we changed our job descriptions to include some form of Agile as a required skill and started hiring every new leader and team member with these skills. Changing job descriptions is often overlooked because organizations are rooted in their usual routines and don't really think about this needed change. You do not want to continue to hire the old skill sets and be in a constant state of training, when you can hire in the new skills to accelerate the transition.

To begin, we embedded experts in several of our teams. We provided scrum training and certification for all team members. As each team acquired these new skills, saw success, and transitioned fully to scrum, we documented our early successes and then repeated the process for the next teams.

We monitored our progress through daily stand-up meetings ("daily scrums"). These meetings keep people informed, aligned, and focused. They are fifteen minutes long, are done in the morning, and are conducted with everyone on the team. Three simple questions are asked every day for each person on the team to address:

- What did you accomplish yesterday? (This updates everyone on tasks that are completed and shows who met their agreed-on commitments.)

- What will you do today? (This updates everyone on tasks planned for the day.)

- Are there any blockers or impediments? (This allows for issues to be discussed and/or resolved.)

The purpose of the meeting is to gain alignment and clarity on project progress, and it holds everyone accountable for their daily outcomes. You will find that some team members have not carried their weight in the past, and this process exposes any weaknesses in the team. It's a powerful accelerator.

Moving to scrum is one step in creating a new and vibrant culture where teamwork is paramount, teams are empowered, and outcomes become more visible. It does require a significant shift in mindset from your people, but once underway, the flywheel takes over. Whatever process you choose, it needs to be collaborative and empowering. Overall, we managed to move the transformation much quicker than we anticipated—instead of it taking a year, we did it in eight months!

Transforming the Platform

When I joined Intuit in the ProTax business unit, our online application performance was substandard. It was at 87 percent uptime with an 8–15 second page load time. Yikes! If you go to a website and find it down, or if it performs slowly, you're only one click away from going elsewhere—and this was happening to us. The industry today dictates a 99.999 or high availability uptime. We needed to achieve two-second response times.[14] We had to make dramatic changes if we were to meet the online industry standard.

We started by setting two aspirational goals: (1) achieve 100 percent uptime availability; (2) achieve less than two-second page load times. This meant we had to do things very differently, so much so that my operations manager at the time walked into my office, closed the door, and said to me, "Mamie, I'm going to give you some feedback."

I stopped what I was doing to listen.

"You can't talk to the team that way," he said. "We'll never achieve these goals. It's not possible."

My response was one I use again and again: "I certainly understand how you feel, and up until now, that might have been the case. But these are your new goals, and my expectation for you and your team is to begin immediately developing your plan to meet these new goals."

People will have different reactions to you setting aspirational goals, and my operations manager at the time certainly did. But you need to be clear and consistent about your goals and never waver from what you expect from everyone.

> You need to be clear and consistent about the goals and never waver from what you expect from everyone.

---

14   Solar Winds, "What Is Uptime? - It Glossary," SolarWinds, accessed December 18, 2023, https://www.solarwinds.com/resources/it-glossary/uptime.

Technology Foundations

To make significant improvement on any platform, there are several elements that require focus along with dedicated resources.

One element is legacy, which you will find in any organization in any field. You must deal with legacy, whether it is a physical platform, software, infrastructure, code, etc. Legacy technology platforms and code are very difficult to update or remove because it's what runs the business. It expands over time and becomes more difficult to maintain and add on new capabilities. Teams are expected to know the legacy technology while also expected to embrace and implement new technology. This is typical in most companies. While some companies manage their legacy technology well, I would say most do not.

One of the hardest things to do is convince an organization that it must prioritize and invest in continually upgrading and improving its technology. This can be an arduous task, because most organizations want to focus on the shiny new projects, not maintaining the old. If you do not focus on legacy improvements to your architecture, your code and infrastructure over time will become brittle and unstable. When application issues arise, technology teams are pushed to apply quick fixes or "Band-Aids" to the problem, which compounds the legacy issues. I call this the "gordian knot," which is a metaphor for a very difficult problem that needs to be unraveled through creative thinking "outside the box." You must work to prioritize your development portfolio with a balance that includes a focus on maintaining legacy technology against the organization's large appetite for endless new projects.

Over my career, in every company where I've worked, upgrading and improving legacy technology was always a key priority because it improved not only customer experiences but avoided the downward spiral of having to address issues related to Band-Aid after Band-Aid fix. In every company it was always a tough discussion and required a lot of persistence. It is well worth the fight!

Another element to platform transformation is technical architecture. This details the technical blueprints required to upgrade or implement sustainable IT systems within an enterprise. It goes hand in hand with legacy technology as the blueprint helps define where legacy technology needs to be sunset, or where it remains but is better able to be supported. At Intuit, because our online systems were so brittle, one of the first things I did was hire an expert architect who could lay out our technical blueprints and build a road map for the teams to implement our technology improvements over time. This road map was prioritized, with the most urgent issues being tackled first. One such issue was that we were using a software development kit (SDK) for developing and deploying cross-platform rich web applications, which was not scalable and was unsupported by the vendor. So in this case, we had to choose new technology. I relied on the expertise of my architect and other technical leaders to select the right solutions to correct this urgent issue.

This wasn't going to be easy as our timelines were incredibly tight, and this required new funding. Therefore, we had to move quickly. Usually obtaining new funding can be challenging, but because our online application performance was so poor, our leaders were eager to authorize funds in time to begin our technology upgrade. This also required the total rewrite of our website in one year because in the tax software business, any change we made to our architecture or technology had to be ready in time for tax season … a very big risk!

Through our talent upgrades and process improvements we were able to achieve success. As we made headway through our platform upgrades, we documented our progress, proving that we would achieve our goals of delivering industry standard application availability and page load times, which we did. As each improvement was made, this further energized the teams, and we celebrated each success. Using solid data to state and build your case and then show concrete results fosters greater trust and continues to build the flywheel effect.

Trust

Trust is often hard to earn, yet it's the easiest thing to lose. You earn trust by being consistent in what you do, by doing what you say you will do, and never wavering. Do not take your foot off the gas. Meet or exceed your commitments. As you continue to demonstrate results, you will continue to earn trust.

As trust is easy to lose, you need to avoid making missteps, but when they happen (which they will) be transparent and own these, as you do your successes. Have the ability to laugh at yourself and not take yourself too seriously. This builds camaraderie.

> Trust is often hard to earn, yet it's the easiest thing to lose.

Every time you achieve success and deliver what you promised, there will be fewer questions in the future. It's magic when this happens as you become more confident to stay the course. People will move from skepticism to support, and you will stop hearing quotes like, "We can't!" and start hearing people say, "Can we do that again?"

Transformation on All Themes

You might recall that, in the beginning, we highlighted eight themes that needed to be addressed. I listed them at the beginning of this chapter, but here they are again (with the order changed slightly with the three most important themes at the beginning).

1. Talent (people)
2. Development and release process (process)
3. Infrastructure (platform)
4. Communication and collaboration
5. Innovation
6. Speed-dedicated teams
7. Application performance
8. Incident management

While addressing the three themes of People, Process, and Platform is the focus of your initial transformation, you will begin to see positive outcomes on the other themes in unexpected ways.

As an example, at the end of our off-site, when we were all aligned to tackle our People, Process, and Platform themes, one gentleman raised his hand and asked a question.

"I know we didn't pick it, but if possible, I'd like to drive the innovation theme for the organization."

We all agreed this would be a great idea, and others in the team joined in to offer help and support. While I was putting focus into setting goals for People, Process, and Platform, I was also working in the background to support our innovation efforts and the other remaining themes. I'd bring these into the fold without it being obvious. Innovation was, in fact, core to our transformation efforts— so much so that we devised an innovation initiative that became key in driving dramatic change.

We will address this in the next stage of the transformation journey: Commit to Stay the Course.

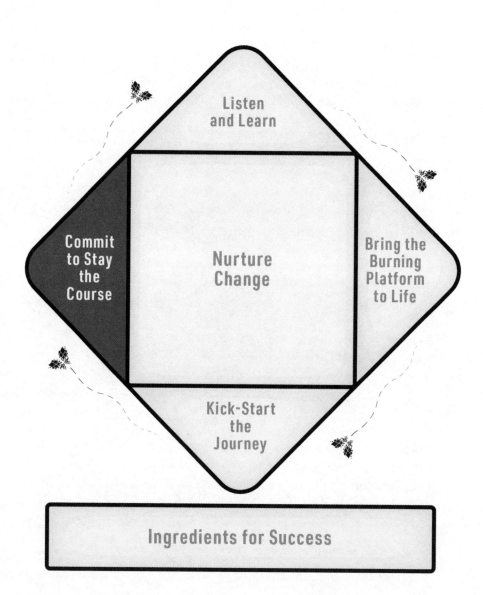

CHAPTER 5

Commit to Stay the Course

*One way to keep momentum going
is to constantly have greater goals.*

—MICHAEL KORDA

Operational Mechanisms for Change

The flywheel has begun—and it's time to accelerate the momentum.

One of the first things I did when I joined Intuit was dial into our software implementations calls. These would begin around 10:00 p.m. to ensure that the website could be taken down without impacting customers in multiple time zones. I joined anonymously in the beginning—I didn't want to cause alarm and just wanted to listen in and understand their release and fallback processes.

In the first call I joined, they worked all night and ended at 6:00 a.m. Despite all their efforts, they could not finish and implement the new code within the release window. In addition, there were no automatic code rollback procedures, which is considered standard practice. By 6:00 a.m., when the implementation had not worked, they needed to scramble to get the site back up and functional for customers.

Once they had the site up and running, at that point I interrupted.

"Hi, everyone," I said. "This is Mamie, and I've been listening to your call tonight. I'm sorry that you were unable to launch this release. For those of you who need to get some rest, go home and sleep. When we get back in the office together, we will review what happened and what we can do to improve our process."

The reality was there were no clear goals and objectives for improvement. From that point on, when I would join the software release calls, they knew I was evaluating their procedures and abilities to release software. I asked questions as they implemented the release so I could learn their thought process and understand where they were falling short.

Because our talent was primarily desktop focused, they did not have the experience in launching web applications or rolling back code releases in the event of issues. The more I spent time with them, the more we were able to speak more openly about their challenges. Eventually they confessed they didn't have all the knowledge and experience to seamlessly launch code, and they were tired of being up at night doing these releases. This was not productive for them, and it was negatively affecting their personal lives.

As with hiring our expert in IT architecture, I hired my expert operations leader who stepped in and started to build the plan for improved IT operations. We collectively agreed to define a grand challenge to move from nighttime to daytime deployments. But this would take some time.

To do this right, we needed a controlled and low-risk deployment strategy. We were running our applications in a data center at the time (not yet ready for cloud hosting), and we laid out a plan to run what we call a "Blue/Green" environment, which is a deployment strategy where you create two separate but identical environments.

One environment (Green) is running the current application version, and one environment (Blue) is running the new application version. This allows you to launch new software without any interruptions to your website operation or to your customers. You test the Blue environment vigorously, and if the new version changes are solid, you switch traffic from Blue to Green. If, by chance, you do encounter any issues, it is a matter of flipping traffic back to Green in a matter of minutes.

Moving to this kind of deployment process took an enormous amount of work, but our operations leader had successfully built this type of environment before, and because of his experience, we were able to make this significant transformation to daytime deployments. Yet again, getting the right talent into my leadership team from the beginning was a big factor in this success.

When we announced that we were going to make this switch and change our environment significantly, there was some pushback from the team. They were skeptical because they had never experienced how to do this type of significant change before. Yet, while it made them uncomfortable, the fact they might be able to do daytime deployments instead of the arduous launches they were used to made them open to this idea, but it meant people would need to learn new skills. Some would rise to the occasion, while others decided they didn't want to tackle this change and left the organization. I understood all these challenges, but we knew this type of dramatic change was necessary if we were going to be more efficient and productive, add better value to our customers, and improve the quality of life for many of our employees. They needed a healthy work-life balance, and we were committed to making it happen.

We established these goals for all our operations team members. We documented the current state of our systems and infrastructure, which gave us the data to measure each improvement, as we made progress toward our goal. While there was still some skepticism, there was also excitement over this new possibility of changing the way we did our releases. As progress was made over time, we used our weekly newsletter to highlight progress. (I will cover details of our newsletter in the next chapter.) This gave the operations team a sense of pride to see their accomplishments shared across the organization—a new experience for them due to the reputation they created from the many challenges experienced in the past.

This initiative took courage and persistence. In fact, the change was fully implemented in about a year. Once we had fully deployed the new environment and produced dramatic results, the operations team was overjoyed. It literally changed their lives. I was told, "We didn't believe this was possible, but this is the best place to work!"

This was a complex goal to undertake. We set the goal and changed the environment—but to get to that point, we had to commit to stay the course and not waver in the face of challenges. We had to fight to get this work prioritized. Even more, it was not only the process that had changed, complete with the employee work-life balance benefits, but the *people* had changed—and ultimately, so had the culture of the organization. This also contributed to the most important goal of delivering more stable and reliable applications for our customers.

It's Not Once and Done

Transformation is not a "once and done" initiative. You must be constantly looking for ways to drive the flywheel forward. You are not just moving the organization from point A to point B but working to change the culture and complexion of the team so they can adjust as new technology develops, new trends arrive, and the market landscape changes. Our CEO, Brad Smith used to have a saying: "You need to repair the roof while the sun is shining." If you wait until the rain begins, your task ahead will be messy. When things are going well, that's the best time to be shoring up what you have and looking for the next innovations and ideas.

> Our Intuit CEO, Brad Smith used to have a saying:
> *"You need to repair the roof while the sun is shining."*

Your organization needs to commit to always looking forward and persevering down new avenues. In the nine years I was at Intuit, we transformed our technology three times. The same was true at Travelocity. In my tenure there, we needed to constantly meet the rapid changes of the emerging internet technologies. Think even about how technology has changed in the last decade. New ideas and innovations continue to push organizations to upskill their talent and skills. Encouraging your teams to investigate new innovations and technologies and explore new ways of thinking is how you keep your teams motivated in the organization. As you build this new culture, it is very rewarding to see teams deliver on capabilities they never dreamed possible, all the while gaining the respect of not only their fellow team members but others across the company, as you publicize their successes.

Operational Mechanisms

To stay the course and continue to transform your culture, there are three key operational mechanisms I use. These build momentum, keep communication open, and monitor how well we are progressing toward our goals.

1. An annual senior staff meeting
2. A quarterly extended leadership off-site
3. A quarterly all-hands road trip

1. Annual Senior Staff Meeting

This is a two-day off-site that takes place at the start of the year with my direct staff. The objective of the meeting is to assess the current state of our talent, process, and technology, to analyze what has worked and what needs our focus in the next one to three years. Each year we look to set a new grand BHAG, one we are all aligned on as a team and will rally behind.

In 2015, I remember quite vividly going into one of these meetings and debating what could be our new grand challenge. Since our business unit at Intuit was focused on delivering tax software, this came with a high degree of tax law updates, which required a great deal of application maintenance. As tax law changes, the software must be updated for all federal, state, and other government agencies' tax changes. We called this high compliance maintenance. Tax professionals use the software to deliver simple and complex tax returns for businesses and customers. When Congress changes tax law every year (many times in December), we need to upgrade all our applications by January in time for tax season. Some years were more complex than others, but with each year, our maintenance requirements continued to grow and eat up much of our development resources.

We call this running the business (RTB). We looked at our data and began to highlight that we were spending an inordinate amount of time working on this required compliance work, and much less on actually innovating and delivering new capabilities and better value for our customers. In fact, as we looked at the data, we realized that almost 75 percent of our activity was involved with RTB work!

We needed to do something dramatically different to change this trajectory.

So, in keeping with our commitment to stay the course, we created an initiative that would galvanize the team behind a new grand challenge to reduce the RTB work from 75 percent to 25 percent. In my experience, having a catchy "code name" for a massive change helps to rally people behind the new vision and grand challenge. The goal was to switch things, to move from 25 percent of the work being done for the customer to 75 percent in three years. So, we came up with "25 to 75 in 3" as our catchy slogan.

We laid out three approaches to move the dial on 25 to 75 in 3. What's interesting is that one of the approaches addressed a need that related back to our initial eight themes when we started our transformation, and that was "innovation." Up until this point, the policy of the company was that every employee would use 10 percent of their workday dedicated to innovation activities, but this was never a reality because the teams' aggressive workload prevented this from happening. So we decided to set goals for our RTB challenge that would also address our innovation.

The first goal was that everyone had to deliver at least one innovation per month that targeted the RTB reduction. Each person had to define what they wanted to do and capture the current state. Then they had to estimate what they thought it would take to accomplish what they wanted to do, and publish the results once completed. This formed part of what we called Innovation Days, which I will unpack later in this chapter.

What's important to note here is how strategic our annual staff meetings became. These were meetings that essentially set the tone for our transformation efforts. These could take anywhere from one to three years to complete, depending on complexity. These grand challenges were set by my direct staff, but as we communicated the grand challenge to employees, innovation after innovation emerged from the teams.

2. Quarterly Extended Leadership Off-Site

In addition to an annual senior staff meeting, the second mechanism I use is a quarterly off-site leadership meeting. This is with the broader extended leadership team, which, in my case, was about thirty people. This is an all-day meeting, and the objectives focus on building leadership capability, progress toward our goals, and talent review. Much goes on in this meeting, so I will take you through it step by step.

A. Outside-In Learning

To improve leadership capability, I focus on what I call "outside-in" learning. I typically introduce a leadership book that everyone is required to read in preparation for the meeting. One book I have introduced is *The Leadership Challenge* by James K. Kouzes and Barry Z. Posner, which delves into leadership capabilities and is very thought-provoking. The homework assignment for each leader attending this meeting is to come prepared to share a short PowerPoint that lists their top three strengths and their top three opportunities. They each present to the team what they prepared, and at the end of each of their presentations, the rest of the team is asked to provide feedback. This requires courage on the part of the leader, as they are being asked to be vulnerable in front of the team, sharing their view of themselves. It reveals their level of self-awareness and can be emotional but an uplifting experience.

The feedback from the team is encouraged to be candid in the form of agreement or disagreement, highlighting examples if there is disagreement. This also requires courage from the team as they are being asked to give their peers feedback on their leadership abilities, which is something many of us are not comfortable doing.

Every time I facilitate this portion of the meeting, I get incredibly positive feedback as we together explore ways to improve our combined leadership capabilities. Some receive the gift of "tough love" when corrective feedback is shared, but it is a gift that helps each person grow as a leader and as a human being. I encourage you to try this exercise as it has, on every occasion, pulled my teams closer together and gained us a shared understanding of our collective strengths and weaknesses.

I also bring in leadership experts from outside the organization to inspire and teach us their leadership lessons. I find that a team can lean into change if they are learning about what others have done with great success. We were always asking: What can we apply in our context that has worked elsewhere that will help bring dramatic improvement?

At Travelocity, I introduced Spencer Johnson's book *Who Moved My Cheese?*,[15] which is a great book that demonstrates how to handle change better. At Intuit, I brought in David Marquet, a retired US Navy captain who wrote the book *Turn the Ship Around*, which is about how he turned the USS *Santa Fe*, a nuclear-powered submarine, from the worst submarine in the fleet to the most successful—and award-winning.[16] Listening to his experience and philosophy of leadership at all levels was a tremendous encouragement to our leadership team, giving them a different way of thinking and from a completely

---

15   Spencer Johnson, *Who Moved My Cheese?: An Amazing Way to Deal with Change in Your Work and in Your Life* (London, England: Random House, 1998).

16   L. David Marquet, *Turn the Ship Around!: A True Story of Building Leaders by Breaking the Rules* (London, England: Penguin Business, 2019).

different context. It was exciting and inspiring to hear David's story. I encourage you to read his book.

Bringing in diversity of thought and influencers from other industries was a strategic discipline, and I would encourage you to look for other books and outside speakers to help shape the thinking of your team.

B. Assessing Goals

Also, during this focus meeting, we assess our goals and fine-tune as necessary. Each goal is reviewed using detailed data to show progress against the current state. Where goals are not being met, action plans are discussed and updated; where they are being met or exceeded, we share all of this in our communication mechanisms. Once we conclude our goals review, we then turn our attention to evaluating our team talent.

C. Assessing Talent

We assess the talent in the organization, noting the skills needed to continue to reach our goals. We rank staff by their skill level, behavior, and attitudes. This is where we use the Performance-Values Matrix as highlighted in the previous chapter.

Evaluating your talent on a quarterly basis is an incredibly important activity that needs to be very deliberate. First, each leader comes to the meeting prepared with details on how they have ranked their current team on a scale of one to ten, according to their performance. This is not a subjective exercise. While this may not be a particularly comfortable exercise, we have to see how each team member measures up against the needed skills and behavioral goals. This gives us an overview of where talent is improving or struggling.

Second, we look at the mix of talent in the organization. We ask ourselves if we have the needed engineers, operations experts, security experts, architects, etc. Then we look at attrition across the teams and push ourselves to not automatically backfill vacant positions but first assess whether the position is really needed or if we would be better served to fill a critical skill gap. It is important to review any skill gaps, redundancies, or single points of failure among the teams. We also continue to update job descriptions as new technologies are being adopted and implemented, to better suit the road map ahead.

At one organization where I worked, we realized there were several points of failure where certain individuals carried all the knowledge. If anything went wrong, it fell to this one person to fix the issue. Others simply didn't have the knowledge. One of my leaders in the engineering team told me a troubling story of an individual who, when asked, refused to share his expertise with others on the team.

He smugly propped his feet up on the table and simply said, "I don't have the time to teach anyone what I do. Everything I do here is super important, and if I stop doing it, things are going to go very wrong."

This type of behavior must be challenged. It is an example of a person with a high skill set but a very poor attitude, who needs to move on, as this kind of mindset is corrosive to the team. This created a vulnerability for the organization, and this was the type of gap we would review in our leadership meeting and make it a top priority to resolve.

This exercise also helps to prepare your team in the event you are given the unpleasant task of having to make headcount cuts, which is an uncomfortable reality in many workplaces that many of us have seen and experienced.

The quarterly extended leadership off-site is a key mechanism that keeps the team's commitments alive and re-energized to continue to push the flywheel forward. It also feeds the agenda for the all-hands road trip we have each quarter.

3. Quarterly All-Hands Road Trip

I make it a priority to travel to each location each quarter whenever possible to share with the teams the "state of the organization," progress against our goals, and to recognize teams for the work they do. We recognize great accomplishments and offer a Q&A for teams to provide feedback. These sessions are typically an hour and a half long, with lunch or snacks included.

Delivering company updates in person shows the teams your commitment to the important work they are doing in their specific location. If you have international locations, it's not always possible to travel to these destinations each quarter, but I made the effort to go at least twice a year with the other quarterly reviews done via teleconference.

This quarterly all-hands is important because it brings the teams together face-to-face, and it gets them out of their daily routine.

When we first introduced our grand challenge of 25 to 75 in 3 to the teams, we used this meeting mechanism to share the BHAG, then asked the team for their ideas on how to accomplish this goal. Because we were in-person at each of the locations, we could make this a fun, energizing activity. When the teams first heard this BHAG, their reactions were easy to see. They first indicated that it looked like an impossible task. So to get everyone thinking differently, we brought sticky notes for all team members to write down any idea they believed would help address our 25 to 75 in 3 challenge.

We made sure everyone knew that they could submit as many ideas as they could think of, and they could be large or small. It got everyone to really think how they might contribute to the goal. This proved to be a tremendous success. First, they were being asked to help solve the problem, and second, we collected about three hundred sticky notes after we were finished with the road trip. We had our program management team consolidate the three hundred ideas into three buckets:

1. Big Rock Projects

    - These were ideas that were larger than any one person or team could tackle without obtaining additional funding— more complex projects that had to be prioritized with the broader business unit leadership team.

2. Individual Projects

    - As discussed earlier, we had each team member commit to doing one project per month, no matter how small, that would contribute to the RTB reduction.

3. Innovation Days

    - We set aside dedicated time that allowed teams to experiment with their ideas to deliver something extraordinary for our customers or our internal team members. More on this below.

The three meeting mechanisms mentioned above are the main drivers that keep you and your teams connected and focused. For this reason, they need to be prioritized. There will be times when you will find them inconvenient and the temptation will be to cancel or delay these mechanisms, but stay the course, as it will help to fuel excitement and keep your flywheel moving.

Innovation Days

Innovation Days was initially an experiment, but it proved to be one of the biggest wins we had, not only as a team, but for Intuit as well. While we were focusing on the People, Process, and Platform aspects of our transformation, I was also focused on how we could encourage more innovation as it played a key role in inspiring teams to take risks and drive dramatic change.

If people are going to think differently, they must have time to be able to think. Innovation doesn't come from any one leader but from people who understand both the technology and the business. Your job is to find ways to tap into the incredible potential in your teams. The inspiration comes from the employee who understands the business and technology and has a passion for their ideas. That is where magic happens.

> If people are going to think differently,
> they must have time to be able to think.

As I have mentioned, in the early days at Intuit we gave each person the authority to use 10 percent of their time toward innovation, but as also mentioned, it was rarely used because of the heavy workload each team carried. There were always other priorities. Operational issues must be addressed, sales and marketing teams want to push their priorities, as do the product managers. But you will find your engineers are itching to innovate. So at Intuit in 2015, we decided to introduce Innovation Days to my organization to unleash the teams' massive innovative potential.

We communicated to the broader business unit that the technology team would stop all development for two days and focus solely on innovation priorities. Now we knew this was going to be controversial. Some of the product managers were very vocal about their skepticism and did not support the idea at all. But we were doing the same things over and over without good results, and it was time to do something different. I had to remind my peers that this was to be an experiment and that it was only for two days. They reluctantly agreed but insisted that I couldn't miss any deadline we previously committed to deliver. I knew that missing two days of our development backlog wasn't going to impact any of our committed deliveries. So, Innovation Days was a go.

We laid out specific rules for Innovation Days and each team/ individual had to adhere to these rules for the two days. These were:

- An individual or team had to deliver an internal or customer-facing innovation, and it had to be production ready. There was a wide range of ideas the teams could tackle, and we were not prescriptive about the innovation chosen.

- They had to define the current state and share their hypothesis of what they hoped to accomplish.

- After the two days, they were to be prepared to showcase what they achieved against their hypothesis to our teams and business unit leaders.

We wanted their work to get recognized, so I was successful with enlisting the help of our executive team to participate in the showcase of innovations developed by the team. We set aside two hours at the conclusion of Innovation Days, and every team or individual was given five minutes (think speed dating) to showcase their innovation, what it achieved, and what was improved (speed, RTB reduction, hours saved, customer problems solved, etc.). The results were astounding. From our first Innovation Days, we had fifty innovations that were launched into production that never would have seen the light of day in a product backlog!

I remember one team member so vividly. He was in our Tax Content team. When he did his presentation, he explained, "I've been trying to fix this issue for five years. It's been on the backlog all this time because my product manager didn't think it was important, and it kept getting pushed down." This required a code fix to a function in a tax form that he had to tab through literally 120 times to get through each page. Everyone who updated this form daily had to tab through it every time before it could be submitted. They totaled the number of people who accessed the form daily, then totaled the number of hours it took to update the form every week, and then the number of hours it took over the course of a year. The amount of time expended on this one activity was astronomical. So he paired up with an engineer in Innovation Days, and when the engineer looked at the technical problem, he was able to solve it in an hour!

As he was showcasing this to the audience, the reactions were priceless. They could see, by just this one fix, the magnitude of what was being accomplished by these two individuals. The Tax Content team member felt exuberant. Initially to others his idea seemed inconsequential, but it revealed that even the smallest idea can produce dramatic results. That small change won him respect and helped to start the Innovation Days flywheel effect.

The executive team was able to hear other equally compelling stories: "We saved the customer 10,000 hours!" "We improved the response time by four seconds!" "We improved the environment for the engineers by removing four redundant steps!" "This automation saved two hours of testing each cycle!"

It was an extraordinary showcase. By carefully documenting what we were doing, we were able to demonstrate what could happen if you remove restraints and give teams time to think, then trust in their abilities. Hearing these stories and others galvanized the organization around this new event. You can guess what the executives and the product managers said afterward:

"When can we do this again?"

We started Innovation Days in my engineering organization, but as others across the business unit saw the results, and the recognition teams were receiving, they also wanted to be a part of this exciting event. We had people coming from sales, customer service, marketing, and asking if they could participate to explore their ideas or support others in their ideas. Pretty soon it wasn't just about engineering; it was the entire business unit. As the flywheel of Innovations Days gained momentum, we were able to hold these four times per year and extended each event for a week with the full support of the business unit. Not only did this catch hold in our business unit, but it spread across Intuit as our approach and results were shared.

During a subsequent Innovation Days, another revolutionary innovation was created by Peter Thomas, an engineer out of our team in India. He had an incredible idea related to improving how we tested our web services, using open-source technology. He was passionate about this idea and called it "Karate." Karate started within our business unit, then took hold across Intuit, and eventually became a global hit. His innovation reduced our web services testing time by 75 percent! And the quality was game changing. Today, Peter has spoken at some of the biggest technology forums around the world and has assumed the leadership role of CEO for Karate. It's fantastic how this all started as one idea in our Innovation Days, because Peter was given time to think, experiment, and pursue his passion.

Our Innovation Days were instrumental in driving game-changing results for our 25 to 75 in 3 grand challenge. We kept detailed records of progress. Everybody shared how they were doing each month to help us reach our target. We gathered all the data and in the first year we reduced our RTB from 75 percent to 65 percent. This was a huge victory! By the end of the three years, we reduced our RTB to 50 percent, which was material to the business. These results happened because we declared a lofty target for ourselves, shared it with the teams, got them energized around this grand challenge, and then let them go.

It reminds me of President John F. Kennedy in 1962 declaring that the United States would put a man on the surface of the moon before the end of the decade. There was no proof that it could be done, but he set out this grand challenge to the country, and we succeeded. You don't know exactly how you're going to achieve your goal, but by making a declaration, people will rise to the occasion and find ways to meet bold challenges!

Success Creates Opportunity

In my first two years at Intuit, we had tremendous success transforming our engineering team. As a result, I was asked to lead the Tax Content team, consisting of 150 Tax Content experts. I took this team through the same playbook I initially took our engineering teams through—the playbook I'm outlining for you in this book—listening and learning, conducting a team off-site to delve into their challenges and bring their burning platform to life, and kick-starting the journey.

David McMinn was a member of our Tax Content team when we kicked off our change efforts. He was not impressed. He had been part of the team for over a decade and had, by then, been through numerous change initiatives that left a bad taste in his mouth. He was honest about how he felt. "We've tried all this sort of thing before," he said to me, "and now we're going to go through another change, yet again?"

I understood his point of view. They had been told what to do and how to do their work by multiple consulting firms and were never given autonomy to do their work the way they knew was right. This came across loud and clear in the off-site we conducted. He wanted the entire Tax Content teams to have ownership and accountability of their work, and not be dictated to by those that didn't understand their work or how to do it effectively.

I said to myself, "Be careful what you ask for because this is exactly what you're going to get."

Because this change needed strong leadership, I enlisted one of my leaders to take on this enormous task. Because of his success transforming our quality assurance testing team, I knew he was up for the challenge.

The first thing we pulled the trigger on was introducing scrum to the teams. As we had done with the engineering team, we embedded experts to help teach each team the new methodology. We knew that giving the teams ownership was the way forward, but making this kind of process change introduced a lot of risk to tax season because the Tax Content team didn't have a full year to implement the change. They were under tighter constraints due to the amount of work that had to be updated. Historically, the team had never been given this kind of end-to-end ownership before. They went from a task-by-task methodology to owning an entire end-to-end process. Each of our twelve Tax Content teams were given responsibility for the federal agency tax updates and multiple state agency tax updates, and they had to deliver flawless content using this new approach.

David was beginning to see things with fresh eyes. We had embedded engineers into the teams to help alleviate and to accelerate any technical issues encountered. As they were learning scrum and the new end-to-end methodology, they were clearly excited to be given the new opportunity to work with engineers directly and own their outcomes. David was becoming more energized. At one point, there was a particular function his team wanted to change. The problem was that changing it was a big risk to tax season because the timing was difficult. Innovation Days was coming up, and if they changed the code as part of it, they risked not being ready for tax season as the change they were wanting was very complex.

"We have this idea," he told me, "that will dramatically reduce our RTB and save us hundreds of hours of work, but it's risky. There is a chance that we won't be ready in time for tax season. We think we can do it, but we don't want to embark on this change if you're not on board. But we're willing to take the risk if you are."

What a difference from before!

"Dave, go for it," I said. "I bet you guys will figure out a way to make this happen."

They locked arms, believed in themselves, and went ahead. Talk about courage! Best of all, they succeeded! Their innovation literally saved thousands of hours of development time. David and his team were able to showcase their results to the executive teams after Innovation Days and we also published the results in our weekly communications, which went across the company. David and his team received empowering recognition—they all experienced a proud moment and a huge sense of accomplishment. Because we publicized their story and the risks they took, it encouraged others to do the same, saying, "If they can do it, so can we."

"You know," David said to me afterward, "I didn't know if we could actually do this. Initially when you came to lead our team, I thought 'This woman doesn't know what she is talking about.' I had lost enthusiasm for my job and was not motivated at all. In fact, I hated my job. But now I love what I'm doing. I'm having so much fun. I can't thank you enough for everything you have done. You've made this a great place to work!"

You can see here how, ultimately, transformation is about building relationships. As the renowned book on the subject, *The*

Leadership Challenge, states: "Leaders never make extraordinary things happen all by themselves. Leaders mobilize *others* to want to struggle for shared aspirations, and this means that, fundamentally, *leadership is a relationship*."[17] To keep the momentum going and stay on your course of change, embrace the mechanisms above and think of ways to inspire your teams like Innovation Days or other events appropriate for your company or industry. Communication is key, and personal face time with employees is critical.

So, what are other ways to raise the engagement and excitement of your teams? How do you keep the relationships at the forefront? The last pillar of the transformation journey, Nurture Change, will answer these questions.

---

17   James M. Kouzes and Barry Z. Posner, *Leadership Challenge: How to Make Extraordinary Things Happen in Organizations* (Hoboken, NJ: John Wiley & Sons, 2017), 57.

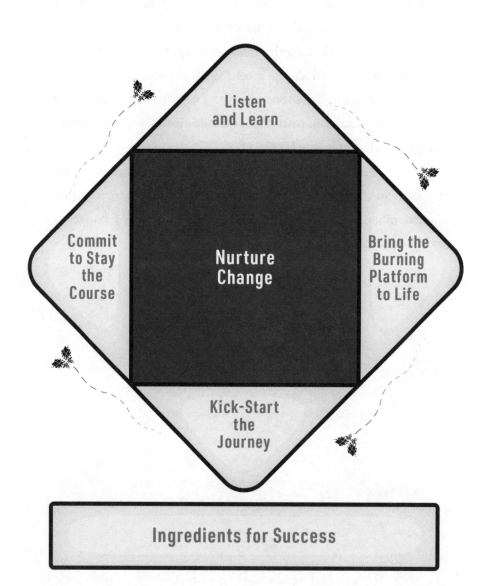

CHAPTER 6

Nurture Change

When you listen, it's amazing what you can learn. When you act
on what you have learned, it's amazing what you can change.
—AUDREY MCLAUGHLIN

As I have been writing this book, my mind fondly recalls the names, faces, and lives of those people I worked with who truly impressed me with their passion, skill, and approach to everything they did. Many of these people have told me, in the years afterward when we've been able to put some time aside to catch up, how much I impacted them, and I often think of how much they impacted me. We did great work together. And, even more, we grew as human beings.

Leading extraordinary change will bring you many rewards that will last a lifetime, but this can only be experienced if you take a very intentional, personal approach to how you lead. I have often repeated the adage, "You hire employees, and *people* show up." When you embark on any significant change that affects people, you must do this with enormous care to achieve the results you seek. This is why the final phase in my playbook, Nurture Change, is the most important.

Nurturing change should be integrated in everything you do. If you look at the Lead Extraordinary Change model, you will note how Nurture Change sits in the center. The arrows on the outside represent the cyclical nature of each phase in the playbook, and they revolve around Nurture Change. You must continually cultivate this skill of nurturing change regardless of where you are in the playbook. It's the glue that binds everything together. Why? Because when you nurture change it truly changes *people*, and when people change, the culture of an organization is transformed.

What "Nurture Change" Means

How do you create a culture where people want to come to work every day for the camaraderie and the teamwork? It starts by treating employees as the people they *are*, who come from different cultures, backgrounds, religions, values, etc. No one wants to be treated like "a number." They want to be treated as valued individuals. It's only when you do this that you can move forward together as a *team* and accomplish great things together. That's why this part of leading extraordinary change is about getting to know people in a genuine, caring way. This can't be contrived. You can't be phony. Most leaders spend little time doing what it takes to develop and nurture people, but doing this creates a long-lasting, healthy culture. Nurturing individuals and teams, as you do your family, is the most powerful thing you can do—and it costs you virtually nothing.

When you understand what motivates people to show up for work every day, you begin to figure out how to get the best version of them involved in what you are building together. You want the best work environment for them, and you can often do that by supporting them in small ways that mean so much. When people know they are valued and recognized for the work they do, it makes a big difference in how they approach their work. This is essentially the heart of what nurturing change is all about.

> You hire employees, and people show up.

Three Ways to Nurture Change

I have three broad categories that reflect the heart and philosophy behind nurturing change, and these will get you started in your thinking about how you can begin to nurture change in your organization. These strategic practices keep me personally connected to the people in my organization and sets them up to succeed. Nurturing change incentivizes people to bring the best work of their lives to the workplace, and that, in turn, contributes the same to the team, with a passion to see the whole organization succeed. The three ways are:

1. Recognize people publicly, coach them privately.

2. Make the workspace fun.

3. Be personal—and listen!

1. Recognize People Publicly, Coach Them Privately

The famous football coach, Vince Lombardi is often credited as saying, "Praise in public; criticize in private," which has become ubiquitous advice. I like to say, recognize people publicly but *coach* them privately. The private meetings are not always negative but can sometimes be very positive as you help someone refine a skill. Even if it's challenging feedback, it's about building people up to reach their potential.

I learned what it meant to be coached privately by one boss I remember well. I had a fantastic relationship with the VP at Travelocity. One day he brought in someone new and introduced him with a glowing review—he was an exceptionally smart architect and systems engineer, and I was looking forward to meeting him and getting to know him.

However, in one of our meetings together, he did some things that really rubbed me the wrong way. He continually cut me off and basically shut me down, and I didn't think what he was bringing to the table was really that extraordinary. After the meeting where he cut me off, I went to my boss aggravated, and told him that I needed to speak about his new hire. What I got in reply completely shocked me.

"Get out of my office."

"Bu—" I interjected, to no avail.

"Get out of my office!"

I left absolutely dumbfounded. I enjoyed a fantastic, transparent relationship with my boss. I trusted him and was always able to speak to him about anything. Why on earth was he responding like this?

I spent the entire day in a daze, stewing on this interaction, going over each and every detail carefully. I just couldn't understand it. I didn't feel I deserved that response at all.

By the end of the day, I sheepishly went back to try and understand what was going on.

"Sit down," he said. So, I did.

"Mamie," he pointed out, "there are two kinds of people in this world. There are those who can change, and there are those who cannot. This new hire of ours is brilliant, and he is going to do wonderful things for us. He has been doing what he has been doing for a long time and isn't going to change. You, however, *can* change. So you will need to figure out how to work with him because, Mamie, he is not going away."

I left knowing what I needed to do, but certainly not wanting to do so. Nevertheless, I met with the new hire. We sat down, and I told him exactly what I was struggling with—the aspects of his personality I didn't understand, the difficulties I had with what he was bringing to the table. He sat there, shocked, and apologized.

"Oh no, Mamie, that's not what I meant when I did that," he said. "It wasn't my intention at all when I said that to you ..." and the list went on.

I realized that I had interpreted the events incorrectly. It was a defining moment, and the two of us became exceptionally good friends after this. If I had not received that candid, private coaching from my boss, I would not have gained the self-awareness I needed to understand my own contribution to the difficulty I was facing, and I would not have found a way to work well with someone who was absolutely brilliant and who I could learn from. I've never forgotten that tough love—it was clearly necessary.

A Weekly Newsletter

Public praise makes a monumental difference to individuals and to a workplace culture. It inspires people and greatly increases their confidence. It gives everyone the feeling that they also have permission to take a risk and do something different. It helps to break the thinking that many people have in a company environment where they feel they need to "stay in their lane." They come to know that here, collaboration is welcome, and that even if you fail, you will get positive feedback for trying. People need to know that some ideas are great, but they may just need refining or time to develop. Don't let them give up too quickly!

One of the significant methods I use to share our successes with each other, and praise publicly, is through a weekly note. Communicating individual and team accomplishments against lofty goals is also integral in building momentum. This can be in the form of a newsletter or email, but the important point is to celebrate successes, showcase innovation, and praise teams and individuals personally. It's also important to provide updates on how teams are tackling goals and reaching significant milestones. When people see progress each week, it contributes greatly to keeping the momentum moving on the flywheel.

My weekly note took a lot of time to create, but it was worth the effort and met with much enthusiasm. It wasn't even my idea but arose from a simple need. People in the organization wanted to know what other teams were doing and what they were accomplishing. They had little communication historically and were very hungry for information. I simply responded to this need, and it turned into a wonderful strategic tool.

In the newsletter I shared our progress against goals, achievements being made by other teams, deliverables that were being launched, and training that was available, and I recognized people in teams who were stepping up and taking some big swings. It started to get quite popular after several months, as people on the team started to share it outside our team. I started to receive requests from other employees to be added to the distribution list so they, too, could receive these updates. I can't tell you how instrumental this weekly newsletter was in creating a positive culture around our changes and keeping the work environment stimulating, interesting, and inspiring.

At Intuit, I called our weekly note "PD Tech Talk" ("PD" referring to product development). I would send out my PD Tech Talk every Friday afternoon as a way of inspiring the team and getting them ramped up for the coming week. Here is what I focused on in my weekly note (it may vary from week to week, but you may want to include these elements in your communications):

1. Reaffirm a goal.

2. Provide examples of where people and teams are taking a big swing, trying something, or embarking on a new experiment.

3. Include what was delivered or launched into production.

4. Incorporate customer testimonials.

5. Add birthdays, retirements, awards, births, etc.

6. Include a call to action (or several, if necessary).

7. Announce upcoming events.

Whatever you include, it needs to capture the emotion of your team, which often inspires them to share it with others. This is why including the names of individuals and teams is so important—you want to praise people publicly.

I would send our PD Tech Talk to my teams, supervisors, my superiors, the CTO, the GM, and my peers. Make sure that enough people are seeing it that are either sponsors or key leaders. This also creates transparency around what you are doing. For example, if we were documenting resource management, we would highlight the changes being made and the impacts it was having for various teams. In other cases, we would talk about experiments that teams were exploring to satisfy a key customer need, or showcase one of our events with pictures and highlights. It's a way of showing that we're working hard but also having fun along the way.

Caping Heroes

For each quarter, we had what we called a "hero award," which was given to someone who achieved something outstanding, unexpected, and worth celebrating. As I did my tour around the offices, we asked employees to vote on who they thought should receive the award that quarter. Once all the ballots were in, we picked the winner for each office. During the off-site we would share the story on why they earned this hero award, and we then don the cape on them in front of the room, thus recognizing them publicly. For the winners, it is a proud moment, and when employees see it, they too want to be a winner. As a result, people step up more and more, thus fueling the flywheel.

This is an example of celebrating big and small achievements. When people do their best, it's exceptionally meaningful to show them that you noticed. Do it publicly. But when they need to be coached, do it privately.

Weekly One-on-Ones

Coaching happens in a one-on-one setting. I use this setting in various ways, but my weekly rhythm includes a one-on-one meeting with my direct leadership team. These meetings help me keep the pulse of what is happening across the organization as it relates to our goals, team dynamics, risks in delivery, etc. We will discuss if there are any issues with deliverables that might be late or are facing challenges, review both business and development goals, and work out if anything needs to be escalated. Plus, these are opportunities to work through any challenges they are facing or even performance issues that need to be discussed. It's about staying connected to what it is they are facing at any given time, and never being caught off guard about what is going on.

Quarterly Touch Points

Many organizations will have different methodologies and expectations when it comes to how performance reviews are conducted. Regardless of frequency and the company's methodology, you need to be meeting with your direct staff to discuss their goals, what's going well, where there are struggles, and their opportunities.

I conduct reviews every quarter, or more frequently if performance issues surface. I start with goals and get feedback on how they think things are going. We then move to their development goals, and they share what actions they've been taking and the feedback they're receiving. I share my perspective with them, and based on what we discuss, we adjust the goals as needed.

Because these reviews center on the employee, they can often start slow and be a bit uncomfortable. This is where you want to have a personal, caring approach that puts them at ease. It's good practice to ask them how *they* think they are doing before you provide your feedback. Try to make this review conversational and objective—and you should always take time to recognize their achievements. Model how to listen attentively in these performance reviews and be clear and direct. You don't want to beat around the bush or delay a conversation as it just builds tension between you.

Where someone is falling short, you should have more frequent conversations, either weekly or bimonthly. The more serious the challenge, the more frequent; make sure to have the documentation to support your feedback, and record the outcome of the meetings with the employee.

During this review or any other review, your employee should never be surprised. You cannot shock someone with corrective feedback that should have been given consistently leading up to the review. It's not fair to the employee and does not foster a good working relationship, not to mention that it brings into question your leadership abilities. It also leaves little time for the employee to make any significant adjustments. Feedback should be given on an ongoing basis, whether in one-on-ones or another type of cadence.

Annual Review

The annual review is just part of the cadence of the quarterly review but conducted at the end of the year. We look back over the year to review accomplishments against the goals and where things may have fallen short or big wins were made. This is also the time when new goals are established for the coming year.

Each year I take the opportunity to ask for my direct report to provide me with a personal goal, one that is something I can do in support of them. I do this for each of my direct reports. When I do this for the first time, the employee is often taken aback as they have never been asked to provide a goal for their boss. While they are a little hesitant, they share what they need of me, and I then craft a goal to support what is important to them. I've been asked to move meetings that conflict with software launches, or that conflict with other team activities. I've been asked to allow an employee to leave at 4:00 p.m. every Thursday so they could take their child to elite soccer practice. The requests come in many forms, but most are easy to put in place, and it makes a lasting impact on the employee when you follow through with these simple requests. This is just another way of nurturing your employees. A bit more on this below.

2. Make the Workspace Fun

If you have a work environment that is nothing but drudgery, who wants to get up every day and come to work in this type of atmosphere? But when you have an environment that has enjoyment and pleasure working with others, it helps to balance the hard work. Your personal life is not all drudgery, and we all crave fun and humor in our lives. It is what bonds us together through tough times. So work to make your environment one where people can work and play. There are many ways to make the workspace fun. Here are some of the strategies I employ.

Birthday Cards

When I joined Intuit, I made the effort to send every team member a birthday card with a short, personal handwritten note with my signature. Acknowledging a birthday is an exceptionally valuable practice for creating a positive workplace culture. It shows appreciation and thoughtfulness. It's well worth the time doing this. I had numerous employees come by my office after receiving their birthday card, absolutely touched that I took the time to recognize their special day.

Not only did it make the employee feel great, but it made me feel great as well. I, too, was the recipient of a birthday card every year from our CEO. The first time I received a personal note from him, it really made my day. I felt the same way that my employees did when they received my card. It encourages you to do more.

Social Events

There are specific things we instituted at Intuit that helped to build relationships and collaboration across teams. They were also fun! These mainly revolved around creating events where employees could meet and get to know each other better. You'll be surprised to find that as your team connects over what seem to be trivial events, they find interesting new ways to collaborate on work. So much innovation happens in informal conversations over a pizza or a beer.

During one of my skip level meetings (which I explain in more detail later in this chapter), employees asked me why our headquarters office was able to have a weekly event where food and beer was served, and why our office couldn't do the same thing. Because our headquarters set the precedent, I wanted to be able to follow suit. So, we decided to introduce what we called "Thirsty Thursdays," which was a weekly get-together at the workplace starting at 4:30 p.m. It started with just our technology team, but then marketing, sales, and other teams heard about it and wanted to join as well.

Our senior leaders initially felt a little uncomfortable with this because there was alcohol involved, but we set some reasonable guidelines around this event, and we launched and then monitored. This ended up being another big win, as people came together and discussed projects, ideas, built new relationships, and just had some fun. There were so many positives that resulted from this one idea. In the end, people really cared about these times together, and we never encountered any issues. But the collaboration that came out of these times was extraordinary.

Competitions

We would also host regular competitions within the engineering department. This was an opportunity to "show your chops" in a fun and competitive environment. Think: hack-a-thon! There was food and strong camaraderie as we set out to see who was going to be the best this time. People really enjoyed the challenge, and it brought people together in new ways.

Pizza Lunches

Another consistent activity we did in the office were "Pizza Lunches," monthly lunch get-togethers over pizza. The beauty of these was they were informal but also intentional in nature. To begin the pizza lunch, I would help kick off the conversation, having everyone go around the room and introduce themselves. They give their name, how long they have been with the company, what project they are working on, and then tell something unique about them that no one in the room knows. This gets everyone to speak, and everyone learns something new about their team members. Plus, there is always a little humor sprinkled in these introductions!

It always amazed me how many interesting conversations emerged between members in these pizza lunches. Someone might mention something interesting they read, or a challenge they're dealing with, or an interesting thought, and someone else would say something like, "Hey, I worked on that before; let me show you what I discovered! Let's take it offline after lunch and see what is possible." It was quite remarkable.

When the employees introduce themselves and share the one unique thing that no one in the room knows, I hear a lot of personal aspects of their lives I didn't know before. People don't normally talk about their family or personal things at work, but it is a great ice breaker in this meeting, and it's fun to see the interesting things people are willing to share. It also helps you build relationships with all the front-line employees. You learn their names, something unique about them, and, for them, you become more approachable and more like their fellow employee—and not an executive nobody knows.

I was quite deliberate about who I invited to each pizza lunch. Here are some important guidelines:

- Invite no more than fifteen people (ten to twelve is ideal).
- Make sure the team is diverse—both men and women, different seniority, skill levels, functions, etc.
- Make the pizza lunch an hour long.
- Make sure you have good pizza!

People love food—and who doesn't like pizza, after all? Hospitality has a unique way of making people feel relaxed and open. People really appreciate it if lunch is on you. It's such a simple thing to do that goes a long way.

A Fun Environment

I remember there was one project where the entire team had to rally to meet a very aggressive delivery. We all needed to put in significant hours to reach an important goal over a six-week period. It was stressful for the teams as they were working late into the evenings. We asked the team if they could make this important deliverable, what could we do to recognize their incredible efforts. I was surprised to hear the same request come up several times:

"We want a shuffleboard."

This was an easy way to satisfy the team's request. My leadership team got together and agreed that we would get the shuffleboard if the team reached the goal. Well, they reached the goal, and we had the shuffleboard delivered. It became one of the focal points in the office where people would take their breaks and have shuffleboard competitions. I would often hear cheers from the shuffleboard area when walking through the office and would poke my head in to see who was winning.

3. Be Personal—and Listen!

One of the best illustrations of how the personal goals and needs of your people, and the organization's needs meet, was revealed to me when I went to India in 2017 to meet our offshore team located there. I met with my key direct report who was new to the role. In our one-on-one, I wanted to know what his specific challenges were. When working through development goals with him, I asked: "Now, what's a personal goal you can give me to support you better?"

I saw the surprise on his face. I could almost read his mind. "What? You're actually asking me that?"

After a few moments of thinking about it, he responded. "I'd like to not have meetings on Fridays and Tuesdays, if possible," he said. "The Friday meetings are our Saturday."

I realized he was right. We were scheduling meetings on Fridays, and that was cutting into his weekend.

As the conversation unfolded, I realized that the team in India was working incredibly difficult hours to make up for the time zone difference between the US and India (a difference of about eleven hours). They were basically working during the US time zone. Teams in the US would schedule meetings for the times that worked best for them, not really understanding the toll it was taking on the India team. The initial role of the team in India was to augment our existing teams, which really meant they didn't own any projects end-to-end. We hadn't considered the impact this was making on our India team.

Every time I visited India, which was two to three times a year, I noticed during our pizza lunches and skip levels that the theme of taking full end-to-end ownership of projects kept surfacing. I knew we needed to make some adjustments. To begin, we decided to move a couple of projects to the team so they could do their work in their time zone. It took us time, but over several years we were able to make a complete shift from staff augmentation to eventually giving the India team full ownership of products end to end. This was difficult for some in the US to accept because they wanted to maintain ownership of these projects, but in reality, there was more than enough to go around. I realized the pushback from some of the teams was mostly just a reaction to change. But listening to our team in India sent a message to everyone: we hear you and we will adjust.

Listen to what people are saying. You might not be able to implement all you hear, but you can start small and build from there. When you do this, you build trust in the organization. If you are making progress and implementing even the smallest of things, people take notice. They can see things are going to get better. It motivates them and gets them to trust you even more when taking bigger risks.

> Listen to what people are saying. You might not be able to implement all you hear, but you can start small and build from there.

Drive-Bys

Another potent tool you can put in your toolbox is doing what we called "drive-bys." This is where any employee comes to your office unannounced to address some questions, an issue, or a request for help. The reasons can be many, but the point is that you are open to productive interruptions. If I was in my office and the door was open, people knew they could "drive by" and have a quick discussion. The term "drive-by" really took off and evolved over time to refer to any spontaneous catch-up with someone or a team at their workspace. As simple as it sounds, our intentional way of doing this had a big impact.

We would find ways to make it fun as well. For example, we would have "Ice Cream Fridays," where myself or several members on the leadership team would push a cart full of ice cream and arrive unannounced, walking through the workplace handing out the goodies. This created a quick moment where we could catch up with people as we went area to area to hear their stories and accomplishments. Since you go to the people rather than the other way around, it feels authentic, and it's a fun ice breaker for a Friday afternoon.

The way I spend time with my teams is quite different from how many others might do it. Many people claim to have an open-door policy, but their door is either shut or they're never present. Even in our day and age of remote work, you'll be amazed how important presence is. You've got to be there, in person. Studies show that social connection is vital for improving our emotional and mental health. Dr. Emma Seppala, author and science director of Stanford University's Center for Compassion and Altruism Research, says this:

> People who feel more connected to others have lower levels of anxiety and depression. Moreover, studies show they also have higher self-esteem, greater empathy for others, are more trusting and

cooperative and, as a consequence, others are more open to trusting and cooperating with them. In other words, social connectedness generates a positive feedback loop of social, emotional, and physical well-being.[18]

Drive-bys might seem like a small thing (and this may tempt you to "try it tomorrow"), but in fact they are incredibly strategic. It's also why my visits to India were so important, both for the team and I. Being there established trust and mutual respect—imperative for doing good work together. It's also why I would visit each of my remote offices and do drive-bys.

Skip Levels

Skip level meetings, which I did monthly, are another ideal time to take the pulse of the organization. My skip levels have some basic requirements:

- Include ten to twelve people.
- **Do not** include managers.
- Strive to have a representative from every different function in the group.
- Have multiple seniority levels represented.
- Have a healthy mix of male and female (in the beginning, we didn't have many females, and we worked to rectify that).
- Schedule for one hour.
- Everyone must participate.

---

18   Emma Seppala, "Connectedness & Health: The Science of Social Connection," *The Center for Compassion and Altruism Research and Education*, March 23, 2023, https://ccare.stanford.edu/uncategorized/connectedness-health-the-science-of-social-connection-infographic/.

Start these meetings by asking, "What's going well? What's working?" Then the second question: "What would be the one thing you'd like to see changed?" or, "Think about what is a challenge for you right now, and what would be your recommendation to correct it."

Everyone is asked to provide feedback. This is an important point. I know some people don't like to talk, or are self-conscious in meetings, while others can dominate the conversation. But you need to give everyone a chance to speak so that all thoughts get airtime.

Listen and learn. This is an opportunity to understand what is going on in your team and observe the meeting dynamics. See who takes all the air out of the room. See who is thoughtful in their responses. Look for body language both positive and negative and make note of this.

From these discussions I always pick up interesting nuggets that can be implemented without difficulty or increased budget. When we can make improvements based on their recommendations, I include these in my weekly PD Tech Talk to highlight what is being done as a result of employee feedback. It's great to show you were listening, and it also demonstrates that a solution was recommended and put into action. As you do this each month, employees come to trust that your motivations are genuine, and their concerns and suggestions are taken seriously. Obviously, there are some things you can't implement due to budget constraints or complexity, but as long as that is made clear, employees understand there is a goal to work toward, and they will feel that the road ahead is positive.

Following a skip level, I share with the extended leadership team what I learned and observed. I do not provide details of who said what but simply share the issues that were raised along with the recommendations and ones that I think we can address. We align on this as a team and put the recommendation in place. If there was a behavior issue observed in the meeting, I will meet with the employee's manager so the development feedback can be addressed with the employee.

Creative Opportunities

There are so many ways you can show people you appreciate them and encourage them to do even better work. When teams deliver or exceed commitments, we would give out either individual or team gift certificates for these accomplishments. We would also give out gift certificates so they could take their spouse, partner, or family out to dinner. When projects get in the way of family time, not only is the employee sacrificing their time, but they are also impacting their families as well.

Including the family in the reward for great work tells the family that you care about their personal life. This inspires the employee to do even better work. Even more, I would often get on the phone and call their spouse, and personally thank them for all they are doing and sacrificing so that we could achieve our goals. That sort of thing costs you nothing, except your time, and yet it can have such a massive impact.

Providing people with gift cards, giving them an overnight package at a resort with their spouse, etc., are spontaneous things you can do for people that are very meaningful and truly incentivize them to do great work and have some fun in the process. The trick is to make it personal. Even inviting people to the pizza lunches or our skip level meetings says that you value their input and feedback, and that incentivizes them to continue to bring their best to work.

Staying Connected

It takes time to do all of this, and you will be tempted to forgo your pizza lunch or ice cream drive-by because there will always seem to be "more important" things to do. My executive assistant would regularly suggest we take these events off my calendar when I would indicate how busy I was. "No," I would say. "You've got to keep it on the calendar. I'm doing that pizza lunch, no matter what!"

You should truly appreciate everyone's input and feedback. It helps to make your environment the best place to work, and that helps your company be a preferred employer in the market. The best talent is drawn to the companies that know how to balance personal and work lives. You want people to look back on these years and say it was the best work of their lives. If they're supported and have the right environment, they can achieve extraordinary things. This will happen through active listening and then acting on what you hear.

The key to nurturing change is *listening and being aware.* I would always have my ear open for what was going on—and you can use the above strategies to keep your ear on the pulse of the organization. If I heard someone's child was sick, or they were diagnosed with a disease—or if they were celebrating good things like their daughter getting married, or their son going to college, or achieving an award in their hobby—I would find them and talk to them, empathize with them, or celebrate with them. If there was something we could do, I would take action.

Having a senior vice president track you down at your workplace and speak to you about something personal in your life makes a powerful impact. Use your weekly communication when appropriate to highlight people and their professional successes, and even mention their babies being born and other public celebrations. People are so appreciative if you take the time to listen and care and be involved.

Many leaders want to focus on results instead of how to inspire teams to do extraordinary things. It's hard to make the commitment to schedule time to listen and engage with employees, especially when you have so many things bombarding you and demanding your time. We all can be stretched but don't give into the temptation to put your ideas for nurturing change on the back burner. Don't let the urgent issues take precedence over building a rich and caring culture. Focus on the people, rewarding their efforts and building lasting relationships. There is a way to do this that builds camaraderie among teams and creates a better workplace, which leads to extraordinary results. You need to carve time out of every day and make it one of your top priorities.

Listen to the heartbeat of your organization. Whatever you do to nurture change, it's about connecting in a genuine way. Find ways to do this at every opportunity. You may not be able to measure each simple interaction for concrete results, but these acts of nurturing change will build over time and create an exceptional culture.

Taking a Break

Leading extraordinary change takes a tremendous amount of energy and mental capacity, which can be draining. Your calendar is full, the days are long, you're persistent in everything you undertake, and there is always more to do. But, as part of modeling the way as a leader, you also need to model how to stay healthy and take appropriate time off.

This is something I needed to learn. There was a time when I was working anywhere from twelve to sixteen hours a day and thought I was absolutely indispensable. This was not a good example. I believed that if I wasn't there, it would not reflect well on me.

At a conference one day, I met Mike Brenner, an accomplished executive coach. I ran into Mike and his wife, Roberta, in an elevator at our hotel. They invited me to dinner, and it was then that I learned he was an executive coach. As we talked, I could tell he was a wise and incredible man. As we got to know each other, I asked if he would be willing to be my executive coach. He agreed, and we made plans to meet up regularly. I explained to Mike that my husband, Ken, wanted me to cut down on the hours I was working to spend more time with him. One day during my coaching session with Mike, he asked me a very simple question: "Mamie, what's important to you?"

"One thing I really wish I could do is play golf with my husband on Tuesdays," I said. "Also, I'd really like my weekends to be mine. I don't want to have to work on weekends."

He asked me what was getting in the way of me doing these things. I didn't really have a good answer, so he gave me two assignments. "You're going to go play golf on Tuesdays with your husband. And you're not going to answer emails on the weekend."

"What?" I said. The mere suggestion to actually do what I wanted made me very uncomfortable.

"And," he said, "you're going to tell your team and your boss what you're doing."

"They'll fire me," I thought.

It was during summer, so we could start a golf game later in the afternoons. Well, being the good student I am, I went to my team that Tuesday and announced: "At 4:30 p.m. today, I'm leaving. I'm going to go play golf with my husband. If there's an emergency, call me, but I will not be looking at email."

I expected this to be a big declaration for the team that would have them protesting or think I'm slaking off. After all, was I not the most important piece on the chess board? Instead, they just looked at me with, "OK, whatever," looks on their faces. I was baffled! "What?" I thought. "This isn't a big deal?"

Then I went to my boss and made the same announcement.

"OK, no problem."

That was it. Everyone trusted me, I trusted them, and it really wasn't a big deal if I wanted to leave early and play golf with my husband once a week. No one batted an eyelid.

My next challenge was to not answer my email on the weekend. I can say that my husband was very excited about this development! Guess what happened after that first weekend? Nothing! No one even cared.

About six weekends later, there was an emergency, and one of my development leaders called me about it. An email was also doing the rounds. After the call, I went ahead and answered the email. On Monday when I walked in, one leader was surprised.

"Wow," he said, "I didn't expect to hear from you this weekend."

I realized the team's expectations of me were altered. By sticking to the plan, they got used to the idea that I didn't answer emails on weekends, and they adjusted. People respected my time because I respected theirs.

What you as the leader do every day is the behavior others will adopt. If you are a workaholic, you will create a staff of workaholics. People speak about leaving your home life at the door when you get to work, but not many speak about leaving your work life at the door when you get home! In truth, both are part of your life, and they affect each other. You need to lead by example and take the time off that you need, which encourages a balance in the workplace.

Taking a break often gets you out of the way so that people can grow and take their own opportunities to the next level. It can be very hard to do when you think you're indispensable, but you're not. A true test of leadership is not how things work when you are there but how things work when you are not. As you empower others to take the reins, it begins to establish your successors, which is what I want to address as I close this book.

Transitioning to New Leadership

In the introduction of this book, I outlined how leadership is not about you. While you will enjoy success, influence, and well-deserved awards for your incredibly hard work and long hours, you will need to implement the final phase of transformation to include what happens when you exit the organization. Transitioning your role is not something that happens overnight. Succession planning takes careful consideration.

Giving other leaders the chance to step in when you're out of the office is crucial in identifying succession candidates. Give over the controls when you recognize leaders have the necessary competency. Take your vacations and give people responsibility. Trust them to do it—and let them shine. Ask for people to step in for you at meetings. When they have a taste of what you are doing, they will not only respect you more, but you can trust them better.

Balaji Mahadev was a leader in our Intuit India team and is a man of incredible talent. He has tremendous technical skill and an uncanny ability to truly nurture people. When you find someone with both these skills, it's very rare! So when the incumbent leader of our team in India announced he was leaving, I wanted Balaji to assume this leadership role. When I announced what I wanted to do to other leaders in India, I got tremendous pushback. Someone else had been waiting for the promotion to director for a very long time, and people thought it was only fair that we give it to them. However, I knew Balaji understood the necessary aspects of the business, was already leading like a director, and was better suited for the role. Eventually he did earn the director position and performed beyond everyone's expectations.

You need to be preparing people for leadership succession to not miss a beat. The same needs to happen when someone needs to step into your role. In my case, I knew exactly who it was going to be because in many ways, they were already doing the job in their division. All they had to do was broaden their responsibilities.

You will need to spend time advocating for people. Good companies trust the leaders to do this well. Some organizations have several committees and endless processes, but I find all these extra steps show a lack of trust and make the process unnecessarily complicated. If you've built trust with your team, they will trust you when it comes to successors.

Evaluate talent by looking at the behaviors that will take the organization to the next level. Give people opportunities to do things and watch what they do. I first look for someone in the organization who can step up to a new role. If you do not have great candidates, don't be afraid to bring in someone from the outside.

> You will need to spend time advocating for people.

The Timeline of Change

Keep the gas pedal down in driving momentum in your transformation. People need to be constantly motivated and inspired. But you have to stay the course and keep things fresh, nurturing the change, otherwise you will stagnate—as will your pace of change.

As I've said, when I begin a transformation effort, it usually takes eighteen to twenty-four months to get into a rhythm. Consistency and persistence are key. You will be amazed at what you can achieve in just a few months and how an organization can evolve with the right playbook! As you hit that eighteen-to-twenty-four-month mark, go back to your team through the Listen and Learn process and capture new quotes of what employees are saying about the organization. When you match these with the old quotes, you can see your amazing progress. Instead of hearing, "I'm stale right now," or "We don't have the skills," you will hear things like I heard at Intuit:

"We have passionate and committed people."

"We are working better together."

"The new infusion of talent is awesome!"

"We are constantly improving."

"We have the right focus on our customers."

"We are starting to drive faster outcomes."

"Love the shift!"

"The opportunity to innovate is awesome!"

During my time at Intuit, our employee engagement moved from a percentage in the low seventies to consistently 85 percent or more! When you're asking people to do tough things and yet your employee engagement is high, it says something! And I attribute it to the strategy that underpins it all: nurturing change.

Remember to look for the ingredients for success. If the ingredients are in place, then be gutsy, take risks, and seize opportunity. Don't be swayed when things aren't going quickly enough. Be tough and persistent.

But most of all, enjoy the journey!

Acknowledgments

To Ken Jones, my husband, who is my biggest fan. He repeatedly provided me with his unwavering support through numerous organizational transformations. He always knew the first eighteen months of any transformation were the toughest and was there for me through each one. He is the best husband, father, stepfather, and grandfather I know.

To my father, George Timmons, who led me down the path of leadership discovery. He loved reading about and discussing leadership dynamics. He was a true mentor as a father, assistant dean of Portland State University professional, and accomplished trombone musician.

To my mother, Margaret Timmons (turning ninety-seven this year), who always told me I could do anything I put my mind to. She has never wavered in her love, support, and incredible words of wisdom. I love her now and always.

To my beloved children, Jason Millard, Amanda Hogan, and Kimberly Millard, who are my pride and joy. They have been with me through all of life's ups and downs and continue to amaze me with their leadership and make me so proud.

To my stepson, Matthew Jones, who I am proud to call stepson. Matt is kind, thoughtful, and generous with his time and, of course, always loves a good joke.

To Greg Schooley, who was the first boss I had that had the courage to give me tough love as a new director in his organization.

He sat me down and gave me coaching that set me on the path to being a better leader and developing better self-awareness.

To Terry Jones, who was an amazing CEO and stood up for me at Travelocity and promoted me to senior VP of technology. If not for him, I would not be where I am today. Thank you, Terry.

To Ravi Metta, who joined me as chief architect for every transformation effort I undertook. Not only did he help drive extraordinary change, but he always supported me through our toughest times—and wasn't afraid to give me needed feedback.

To Vinod Periagaram, who was on my leadership team at Intuit. He was always willing to take on the toughest challenges with the best attitudes. He persevered and drove extraordinary transformations, delivering incredible results. Vinod, thank you for encouraging me to write this book!

To Chris Bradford, who was my HR partner at Intuit and was instrumental in helping me drive change across all teams and all offices. I call Chris my "HR partner with chops"! Thank you, Chris.

To Ramesh Melkote, who was my operations leader at Intuit and was instrumental in driving technology firsts at Intuit and did so in the face of so many challenges.

To Ritu Krishna, who led my program management office at Intuit and who successfully juggled the never-ending number of programs to help us drive successful results.

To Mike Brenner, my executive coach at Travelocity who shared his wisdom and pushed me to learn how to better balance work and personal life. He also taught me that asking for what you need is not something to be afraid of and is not a weakness but a strength.

To Veronica Pouttu, the best executive assistant I have ever had. She is an extraordinary leader who was able to juggle multiple things simultaneously and never drop a ball. She supported my entire team with creativity and with an amazing attitude.

To Brad Smith, who was CEO at Intuit and who led by example and served as an incredible mentor for me and for all the Intuit family. His care and kindness of others is an example that all of us could follow.

To Cece Morken, who led our business unit at Intuit. She provided me with the autonomy to drive the needed transformation without micromanaging. She changed my life when she promoted me to senior VP at Intuit, and I will always be grateful to her for trusting my abilities and leadership capabilities.

To Tayloe Stansbury, who was the CTO at Intuit, and who gave me the autonomy I needed to drive technology change for my business unit and for Intuit.

To Scott Cook, one of the founders of Intuit, who led by example and challenged all of Intuit's employees to connect with customers and experiment without the fear of retribution.

To David Mather, who was the CEO of Hoovers (Dun & Bradstreet) and gave me the autonomy to drive significant technology change.

To Michele Iacovone, who worked with me at Hoovers, then took a lead technology position at Intuit. When my name was submitted to Intuit as candidate for VP of technology, Michele was key in supporting me as a strong candidate with the decision makers.

To Jack and Carol Weber, the most impactful instructors I know in leadership development at the University of Virginia Darden School of Business. I was honored when they asked me to speak at one of their leadership challenge courses, and they taught me to teach their incredible material through their train-the-trainer course. They helped me build my leadership capabilities and I will forever be grateful for their wisdom and their kind, caring approach.

To my editors at Forbes Books, Lauren Steffes and Ryan Peter, for their ongoing support and continued feedback to finally getting my manuscript completed.